Tips For Book Instruc...

Zachariahd B Villaz

Bootcamp Workout Benefits

Do you take pleasure in outdoor activities, strenuous exercise, and socializing with others? You should enroll in a boot program then! Boot camp combines discipline, adversity, and tenacity. It is a full-body exercise that requires the use of all of your resources, and no two workouts are alike.

Body and mind can profit greatly from boot camp. So it comes as no surprise that it is growing and has been sweeping across Europe since 2000.

Where did boot camp start?

As the term implies, boot camp was not created in the Netherlands. In the US military, boot camp first appeared. With the equipment that was accessible at the time—ropes, tree trunks, car tires, benches, and people's own bodies—soldiers were trained in an extremely intensive manner in a brief period of time.

Everything was done to increase your strength and fitness.

Around 1999, boot camp appeared in Europe. The general population accepted it right away, and it is now an essential component of a full-body workout.

There are many benefits to bootcamp, but there are also some possible drawbacks. The most significant ones have been enumerated for you.

Bootcamp is a total-body exercise.

In a brief period of time, you train (almost) all muscle groups. Everything is addressed, including your core, back muscles, pectoral muscles, leg muscles, and arm muscles. It includes both cardio and strength conditioning. Have you been hurt? Then, during boot camp, you can easily skip the appropriate muscle group and concentrate more on others.

Boot training can be completed anywhere.

All you require is some clean outdoor oxygen. You make use of everything you encounter, including playground equipment, a ditch, fences, benches, and a sandy walkway. Cones, skipping ropes, and ankle and wrist weights are all practical items that you can bring (and use to immediately practice running with weight). You can also build up an open area with training aids like speed parachute, agility ladder, wall balls, strength bags, and bulgarian bags.

You exert a lot of energy.

Boot camp is (very) intensive, so you work out many different muscle groups at once, which puts additional strain on your body and causes you to burn more calories. 500 calories can be added to that in just one hour of boot class!

Both novices and experts can attend boot camp.

You can always train at your own level because you use everything that you come across (or can conveniently carry with you) during a workout. There are typically beginner and advanced boot camp training classes available. Workouts can easily be modified to the degree, whether it be more or less intense, shorter or longer training.

Together, you exercise

A boot camp program can, of course, be created independently, but it is typically done in a group. Training with a partner inspires you as you support and urge one another during the tough times. Often, exercising with a friend gives you the additional motivation you need to work out even when you don't feel like it.

You stretch yourself.

Training with others often leads to pushing your boundaries. With boot programs, you frequently take things a step further than you intended. This is due to the fact that you are constantly faced with new challenges, the group supports you, and your desire to go the additional mile to improve your fitness.

Boot training eases tension

Both the body and the psyche benefit from outdoor exercise. the endorphins released during exercise, being outside in the fresh air, being physically active, being around people you can speak to, being in a green environment, and clearing your mind completely. Boot camps instantly relieve tension and infuse you with newfound vigor.

Could Help You Maintain A Nutrient-Rich Diet

Since boot camp workouts are all-encompassing approaches to health and fitness, they also cover nutrition. The teachers may offer printed guides or regular nutritional guidance. On days when you don't work out, follow these dietary recommendations to prevent your body from reverting to old habits and undoing all the hard work you've already put in. You can optimize your diet to make the exercises even more effective and efficient.

May aid in elevating mood

The endorphin release, like any exercise, can be a real energy booster. Endorphins improve mood and eliminate stress hormones from the body after an intense hour-long exercise that leaves you sweating profusely and your blood pumping vigorously through every inch of your body. You will feel energized, ready to face the day, and eager for your next workout.

Many exercise regimens result in this kind of mental clarity and improved mood, but the intensity of boot camp workouts intensifies this impact even more!

Exercise Enhances Happiness

Exercise produces endorphins, as it does with any workout. Your mood will be lifted by the feel-good chemical released in your brain as a result of the bootcamp exercise, which will also help reduce stress.

Additionally, the enjoyment you derive from working out and socializing with your pals will increase your happiness. Being able to exercise with individuals you like and respect greatly improves your mood.

Bootcamp exercises are specifically made to lift your attitude.

It won't ever get monotonous.

Let's be realistic, I mean. It's very possible and probable that your fitness routine will get boring. Particularly if you're spending 45 minutes on the elliptical or machine while glaring at the wall or screen directly in front of you and pleading for the minutes to pass as quickly as possible.

Bootcamp exercises eliminate that chance. Because you never know what to expect, a bootcamp exercise will never get boring.

Every class is unique, and until the teacher instructs you what to do, you have no idea what you'll be doing. There are no two courses alike. Additionally, you are continuously switching between exercises, which limits the amount of downtime you have for boredom.

It's a good idea to attempt a bootcamp workout if you have a tendency to get bored with your workouts easily. It will alter how you perceive the exercise.

Contents

CHAPTER 1: INTRODUCTION

Upon completion of my American Council of Exercise personal training certification in December of 2011, I was offered a job coaching group fitness at a local YMCA. I was given a brand new class over which I could have complete control—format, programming, the works. I was thrilled at the opportunity—and terrified at the same time. I had been coaching at a local CrossFit gym for six months, but I never had to come up with the workouts myself. I never had a class of my own and the thought of programming two classes a week was intimidating. With just a few weeks before my very first class in mid-January, I did some frantic research for some ready-made workouts to help me program my class, but I found nothing out there. I would have given anything to have some help and it would have saved me many stressful nights. I created this book FOR YOU in order to help YOU avoid the same struggle I faced.

Have you just been offered your first group fitness job? Do you lack the experience programming workouts? Are you a bootcamp owner who wants some new or fresh ideas of programming? Are you an experienced group fitness instructor but pressed for time to come up with workouts because of your commitments to your family, your kids, or another job? Are you a personal trainer looking for challenging workouts for your clients or small groups? Are you an individual looking for ideas or some structure to work out at home? Yes? Then THIS BOOK IS FOR YOU.

This book is comprised of actual workouts that I used throughout three years of coaching group fitness. When I started coaching my Cardio Fit class, there were four or five members in attendance. Throughout the span of three years, my class grew in attendance to an average of 30-40 per class, with an all-time high of 62 members, totally outgrowing the group fitness space! Class members spread word of the fun they were having and brought their spouses, older children, siblings and friends to the class. They became faster, stronger, leaner, and more muscular. They gained confidence in themselves and their abilities, and throughout all of that, they had FUN!

Anyone looking for new, fresh, and varied ideas in their programming, or anyone struggling to prepare programming while trying to balance the commitments of family, kids, and job can benefit by having these workouts. Give yourself the freedom and help you need by having this resource available to you anytime.

Just listen to some comments from some members who participated in my workouts:

"Your workouts made me want to find my potential rather than believing that I was at mine."—John C., Louisville KY.

"Alise's CardioFit/Power class was my first exposure with 'Cross-Fit-esque' movements, HIIT, and mentality. She took into consideration all fitness levels when developing WODs and always provided safe alternatives to more complex moves. She epitomized a 'can-do' mantra that empowered her class to grow stronger not only physically but spiritually too. She led by example and encouraged me to set goals, which helped me train for and complete a Spartan Trifecta last year."—Lisa H, Louisville, KY

"Prior to taking Alise's class, I would just wander aimlessly around the gym floor. Her class gave me the tools to aid in my 80 pound weight loss. Better yet, she gave me the confidence to work out independent of a group setting."—David B., Louisville, KY

"I had the pleasure of getting to know Alise a few years ago when I took her class at the local YMCA. Not only is she incredibly knowledgeable about training, but she also has a magic quality that makes you want to push yourself out of your comfort zone, while also focusing on safety. I am in my mid 50's and am now stronger and healthier than I have ever been. Even though we are no longer in the same city, when I take a boot camp type class, I always hear her voice in my head telling me that I am stronger than I think. Alise's workouts are challenging but do-able. It will change your body. I hope that everyone who reads this book will someday have the privilege of meeting this incredible lady in person. She is an inspiration!"—Kathy H., Louisville, KY

I PROMISE you that your students will LOVE these workouts while also getting faster and stronger.

I would have paid much more than the cost of this book when I first started out. Don't miss out on giving your classes some fun, varied, and buttkicking workouts! In addition to 52 carefully programmed workouts, I've also included dynamic warm-up ideas you can use for your class and a detailed glossary describing every movement and exercise used within the workouts. As an added bonus I've even thrown in a chapter of some really fun "themed" workouts that your classes will be talking about for a long time! You can't afford NOT to buy this book.

I know you lead a really busy life and are pulled in a million different directions. I am too. And I just want to do something to help you out when you need it. To take one thing off your to-do list. To give you one less thing to worry about. Wouldn't it be nice to know that when you need it, you can just open up this book and have a workout ready for class? Take control of your life and your time right now. Give your class something new and challenging every single session. Grow your class or your bootcamp and inspire and motivate your members to be the best they can be.

CHAPTER 2: EQUIPMENT

Listed below is all equipment required for the workouts in this book. If you teach a group fitness class or run a bootcamp, chances are you have most of the equipment and space recommendations available to you. If not, use your own imagination and expertise to substitute equipment or just replace it with something similar from a different workout.

Running Space: A round track or an indoor/outdoor space in which members can run around or out and back. The running distances in this book range from 100m to one mile, so it's ideal to have the capability to measure running distance on a track or an out and back line.

Dumbbells (DB): An ideal range of dumbbells for your class range in weight from 5 pounds to 40 pounds. Make sure there are enough dumbbells to be in pairs.

BodyPump Bars and Weights: Many of the barbell exercises listed in this book can be performed by using BodyPump bars and accompanying weights.

Versa Bars: Versa bars, ranging in weight from 4 pounds to 36 pounds. Can be used for the barbell exercises in place of BodyPump Bars, if they are unavailable.

Resistance Bands: Rubber tube type with handles or without, in varying ranges of tension.

Jump Ropes: Adjustable or in varying lengths to accommodate members of different heights.

Yoga Mats: Ideal to protect body from a hard floor or ground during sit-ups and planks.

AbMats: Small mats to protect the rear on sit-ups.

Weight Plates: Barbell weight plates, ranging from 10 pounds to 45 pounds. Ideally made with a "handle" capability.

Kettlebells (KB): Ranging from 10 pounds to 53 pounds. (Ideal but not necessary for any of the workouts in this book.)

Plyometric (Plyo) boxes/Aerobic Steps: For step and jump purposes, aerobic steps ideally ranging in height from 4" and up. Plyo boxes ranging in height from 12" to 24".

Medicine Balls/Slam Balls: Medicine Balls (Medballs or MB) are soft large solid leather covered weighted balls used for throwing, passing, and catching. Slam balls are usually smaller, with a harder shell typically made of tough rubber so it can handle a high-velocity impact against the floor. (Ideally ranging in weight from 10 pounds to 30 pounds for these workouts.)

Weighted Battle Ropes: Training ropes that come in various lengths and thicknesses. To anchor ropes, just loop around a pole.

Tennis Balls: One or two dozen tennis balls.

Deck of Playing Cards

Spin Bicycles: If available but not necessary for the workouts in this book.

Stopwatch/Clock with second hand: To keep track of time intervals as you coach and for class members to keep track of work or rest intervals themselves.

CHAPTER 3: WARM-UPS

I prefer to use dynamic warm-ups for my workouts. A dynamic warm-up is comprised of stretches and exercises that require you to be in motion as you stretch. They are ideal because warming up in motion enhances muscular performance and power. Dynamic warm-ups activate the muscles to be used during a workout. Dynamic stretching improves range of motion, improves body awareness, and prevents injuries.

If space allows, I like to "walk" each warm-up movement across the available space, usually a distance of 15-20 yards, changing each movement with each change in direction. If space or number of members prohibit this, you can do these warm-ups standing in place. I like to start with low intensity exercises gradually increasing in intensity throughout the warm-up.

Airsquats (bodyweight squat): Stand with feet a little wider than hip width apart, toes turned out slightly and arms extended in front. Bend knees slowly, sit hips back and down behind as if sitting down into a chair. Keep the knees tracking over toes and weight balanced towards the heels.

Arm Circles: Stand with feet hip width apart with arms raised at sides. Draw small forward circles with the arms. Reverse direction.

Band Pull Aparts: Stand shoulder width apart. Grab a medium resistance band about 12 inches apart and hold directly in front of chest. Pull the band away from itself until the hands are in line with the body perpendicular from the body and parallel to the floor.

Bear Crawl: Drop onto all fours with hands directly under the shoulders, then raise up onto the feet. Move the right hand and left leg forward simultaneously. Then move the left hand and right leg forward. Make sure the knees never touch the ground.

Box Jump: Stand in front of a plyo box or cardio step. Jump onto box and immediately back down to same position. Immediately repeat. Jump back and forth from floor and box as fast as possible.

Burpees: Start in a standing position. Kick both feet back, while simultaneously lowering into the bottom portion of a push-up. Arms will not be extended. Immediately jump to feet to the squat position, while simultaneously pushing "up" with both arms. Leap up as high as possible from the squat position and clap overhead.

Burpee Broad Jumps: Perform a burpee, instead of jumping and clapping overhead at the end of the movement, perform a squat jump forward. Land, and repeat the burpee.

Butt Kicks: Stand tall on the balls of your feet, hip width apart. Rapidly kick one heel up to your butt, alternating legs. Go fast!

Carioca (Grapevine): Start in an athletic stance with feet hip width apart. Traverse while crossing one foot in front then behind the other. After a specified distance, switch directions.

Crab Walk: Similar to a bear crawl, but facing upwards. Sit on the floor, then lift up on the hands and feet. Crawl in each direction, like a crab.

Dislocates (Pass-Throughs): Start with feet shoulder width apart. Hold a PVC Pipe or resistance band at waist with a wide overhand grip. Keeping arms locked out, bring the PVC pipe/resistance overhead and down to the lower back until it touches butt, return to starting position and repeat.

Fast Feet: Start in an athletic stance with feet slightly wider than shoulder width, knees bent. Sprint in place, with minimal leg raise—emphasis on fast feet.

Forward and Back Leg Swings: Grasping a fixed object (such as the side of a wall) for support, straighten and swing one leg forward and backward. Keep the leg straight and make sure range of motion comes from the hips and not from flexing and extending the lower back. Only extend the range of motion as far as you can while generating the motion in the hips.

Four Square Jump: Jump in an imaginary square box pattern touching each corner of the square with each jump.

Frankensteins: Stand with legs together and both arms extending out in front. Step and kick one leg straight up to the corresponding hand, keeping leg as straight as possible. Try to touch the toe with the hand then return while stepping forward. Repeat, alternating sides. Keep arms high and be conscious to kick "up" to the hand.

Glute Bridges: Lie on back in a bent-knee position with feet flat on the floor and close to butt. Gently flatten the low back into the floor. Keep the abdominals engaged, push through the heels and lift the hips up off the floor. Avoid arching the low back. Squeeze glute muscles and slowly lower back to the starting position.

Good Mornings: Stand with feet hip width apart and place hands at the back of the head with elbows opened wide. Press the butt backward and at the hips, until back is almost parallel to the floor. Keep a slight bend in the knees while bending forward. Return to standing position, squeezing the glutes at the top.

Hamstring Ankle Sweep: Extend one leg in front of you with that heel touching the ground and toe pointing up to the ceiling. Bend forward with straight arms and sweep from the forward foot to the sky while keeping your toes up on your front foot. Repeat the movement, alternating steps.

High Knees: Start standing with feet hip width apart. Lift up one knee so that the leg is parallel to the floor. Lightly jog with high knees going to this high parallel position.

High Knee Pulls: Stand with feet hip width apart. Lift and bend a knee, gently pulling it close to the body. Return and repeat while alternating legs.

Inchworm: Stand with feet slightly apart and bend forward at the hips, touching toes. Extend arms in front of the body and walk forward into the top of a push-up position. Then, walk the feet up to meet the hands in front, keeping legs as straight as possible.

Jog: Slow, easy running.

Jumping Jacks: In a fluid motion, jump legs out to the side and raise arms up overhead. Land and repeat.

Jump the Line: Imagine a vertical line on the floor to one side. Hop over the line with both feet then hop back to start position as quickly as possible. Repeat.

Jump Rope: Stand with feet shoulder width apart, grasping jump rope handles together with both hands in front of body. The rope should hang behind you. Use your hands and wrists to swing the rope over your head. Jump over the rope as it approaches the top of the feet.

Lateral Leg Swings: Face a wall. Place both hands on the wall, and lift one foot slightly off the floor. Swing leg across body to the right, then to the left. Keep torso as immobile as possible.

Lunge: Stand with feet together and hands at the waist. Take a big step forward and bend legs to form 90-degree angles. Return to standing by pressing back up with the lead foot. Keep body upright while alternating legs.

Lunge with Torso Twist: Perform a forward lunge. At the bottom of the lunge, twist torso to the lunging leg side. Alternate lunge, twist torso to the opposite side. Keep hips still and twist from the waist up only.

Mountain Climbers: Start in a plank position both hands on the floor. Drive one knee up towards the corresponding elbow and quickly alternate sides. Increase speed to increase your heart rate.

Prisoner Walk: Start in a deep squat position with hands clasped behind the head. Waddle forward one leg at a time in that squat position.

Runner's Lunge: Start in an upper plank position. Lift and place the right foot to the outside of the right hand and hold the deep stretch for one count before returning to the plank position. Repeat on the opposite side and continue to alternate. Keep the back knee off the ground.

Side Shuffle: Start with bent knees in partial squat, with hands held in front of chest. Shuffle briskly from side to side keeping body low and chest lifted.

Sideways Walk with Squat: Start standing with feet together. Step the right foot out to the side and squat down. Push up and bring the left foot together to the right foot. Continue for a distance and then switch directions.

Spiderman Crawl: Start in the Runner's Lunge position. Bring one hand forward while dragging the opposite leg forward until that knee comes to the forward elbow. Repeat the movement with the opposite hand and opposite leg in order to gradually move forward.

Squat Jumps: Stand with feet hip width apart. Sit hips back and down into a squat position. Jump straight up into the air and land softly back into the squat position. Repeat.

Squat to Stand: Stand tall with feet about shoulder width apart from each other. Then push your hips back, bend at your waist, and grab your toes. Drop hips back into a squat and lift the chest upward while lowering the body towards the floor. Hold then push the hips upward to a standing position while continuing to hold toes.

Standing Quad Stretch: Stand on one leg with knees touching. Grab foot with the corresponding hand and pull toward the butt. Keep chest upright.

Standing Scissor Kick: Stand upright, with feet shoulder width apart. Jump feet forward and back in a scissor motion.

Suicides: Set up four cones an equal distance apart in a straight line. Put them farther apart to increase the intensity of this exercise. Get in a sprint-ready stance at the first cone. Sprint from cone 1 to cone 2 and quickly change direction to go back to cone 1. Then sprint to cone 3 and then back to cone 1. Lastly, sprint to cone 4 and back to cone 1.

Superman to Banana: Lie on stomach with toes pointed down and arms stretched out overhead. Slowly lift knees and arms up into the Superman position. Engage the core and roll to the left or right, using abdominal muscles, not the hips. Roll until you are on your back into the "hollow position," with arms extended overhead, legs straight out.

Walking Lunges: Stand with feet together and hands at the waist. Take a big step forward and bend legs to form 90-degree angles. Step feet together by bringing back foot to front foot. Step forward with the opposite leg and continue. Keep body upright while alternating legs.

Yoga Plex: This is a fantastic little complex by Nick Tumminello. If you are pressed for warm-up time, several reps of this will do the trick. Start in a top push-up position. Push hips up into Downward Dog yoga pose-balance on your hands and feet while raising your hips up and back—you will resemble an upside-down V.

From there, reach your right foot up to your hand into the Runner's Lunge. Keeping weight on your left hand, lift your right arm up, open up to the right side, and with your right arm make a big backwards arm circle. Bring your right leg back to the starting position, repeat downward dog. Then take left leg up to the left hand to the Runner's Lunge, then repeat the arm circle on the left.

Some fun group warm-ups:

Junkyard Dog: The junk yard dog warm-up consist of two parts, each done with a partner. Part 1: Partner A sits on the floor with his arms to the side (parallel to the floor) and legs out front touching each other. Partner B starts behind partner A, jumps over arm 1, turns 90 degrees, jumps over the legs, turns 90 degrees and jumps over arm 2, then turns 180 degrees and repeats going the opposite direction...this is 1 rep. Perform this 5 times, then switch. Part 2: Partner A gets on his hands and knees curls into a tight ball, and partner B jumps over partner A. At this time partner A pikes up and partner B low crawls under partner A—this consists of 1 rep. Perform this 5 times, then switch.

Roxanne or Thunderstruck: To the tune of Roxanne by the Police/Thunderstruck by AC/DC. Start the song and the class performs jumping jacks. Every time the name "Roxanne/Thunderstruck" is sung, class performs a burpee.

Back to Front Sprint (Sometimes referred to an Indian Run): Have everyone line up single file and run a prescribed distance. The last person in the line sprints to the front. When that person gets to the front of the line, the next last person sprints to the front and so on.

Medicine Ball Run: Class lines up single file running a specific distance. First person in line has a medicine ball. That person tosses it over their head to the person behind them and run to the back of the line. Choose a heavy medicine ball.

Pizza Game: Give every athlete an AbMat and have them hold it overhead like a pizza. Then on your yell of "Go!" everyone can begin running around and trying to knock over everyone else's pizzas. You can use a Burpee, Airsquat, Push-up, Sit-up, etc penalty.

Bring Sally Up: to the song "Flower" by Moby. Airsquat on "Bring Sally Down." Stand on "Bring Sally Up."

CHAPTER 4: WORKOUTS

Now the fun part, the workouts themselves. Here are 52 workouts all ready for you to use in class. All of the workouts are around 50 minutes in length, depending on the length of the warm-ups that you choose. Workouts are comprised of 1-4 segments and I've marked these A-D. I believe very strongly that variety in the workouts cultivates more engagement and retention from the class members. I also believe in incorporating strength movements within the workouts through the use of weighted bars and/or dumbbells.

In my experience, athletes often underestimate their strength, so I generally encourage them to go heavier if possible. Finally, I also believe very strongly in the rest intervals written into the workouts. Most of the workouts alternate periods of rest/recovery with periods of high intensity exercises. Athletes can work harder and with a higher intensity after specified rest intervals, leading to quicker gains in fitness level and strength.

Feel free to use these workouts as written, in or out of order, or switch segments around as needed in order to modify for space, equipment, or class size/ability. I know your classes will enjoy the workouts as much as mine do.

Workout #1

Warm-up

Circuit of Stations

Pick 10-15 exercises. Write each exercise in black marker on a sheet of cardstock paper. Tape each card onto the wall around the room or lay each card on the ground in a huge circle. These are your stations. Each person will pick a station at which to start.

(There may be more than one person at a station). Start the stopwatch and have each person perform the exercise for the specified amount of time. When that time interval is up, each person rotates clockwise/counterclockwise as quickly as possible (I call out "Switch! 3, 2, 1 GO!) and the next interval begins. Once everyone has gone around the entire circuit once, rest the prescribed rest period. The length of the entire circuit is contingent upon how many exercises are in the circuit, so scale for the class time period.

For example, the 14 exercises I selected for this circuit are:

- Jumping Jacks

- Airsquats

- Plank Hold/Plank Up-downs

- Sit-ups

- T-Push-ups

- Lunges (weighted or bodyweight)

- Battle Ropes

- DB Step Ups Onto Box

- Goblet Squat w/DB or KB

- Mountain Climbers

- DB Thrusters

- Medball Slams

- Squat Jumps

- Scissor Jump

The time intervals for each round are as follows:

- **Round #1:** 15 seconds each exercise (w/ transitions this round lasts 4-4 ½ minutes)

- Rest 2 ½ minutes

- **Round #2:** 30 seconds each exercise (w/ transitions the round lasts 8 minutes)

- Rest 4 minutes

- **Round #3:** 30 seconds each exercise (w/ transitions this round lasts 8 minutes)

- Rest 4 minutes

- **Round #4:** 15 seconds each exercise (w/ transitions this round lasts 4-4 ½ minutes)

If your class can handle a really challenging circuit, limit the number of movements to 10, and use the following interval pattern:

- **Round #1:** 15 seconds each exercise

- Rest 2 minutes

- **Round #2:** 30 seconds each exercise

- Rest 2 minutes

- **Round #3:** 45 seconds each exercise

- Rest 2 minutes

- **Round #4:** 30 seconds each exercise

- Rest 2 minutes

- **Round #5:** 15 seconds each exercise

Workout #2

Warm-up

A. Cardio Circuit—3 Rounds

Each round consists of the following:

- Two Minute Spin (If you do not have access to spin bikes, then substitute with 2 minutes of jumping jacks or jump rope)

- 300m Run (150m out and back or 300m circle)

- 8 Squat Jumps Across Floor

- 8 Push-ups

- 8 Squat Jumps Back Across Floor

Go back to the start of the circuit and repeat for two more rounds.

B. Strength Circuit—3 rounds

(Upper Body + Lower Body = one round. If desired, increase the weight of DB each round)

Upper Body

- 8 DB Curls

- 8 DB Rows

- 8 DB Presses

- 8 DB Tricep Extension

Lower Body

- 8 DB Squats (hold DB at shoulders)

- 8 DB Lunges (8 each leg)

- 8 DB Step Ups (8 each leg)

- 30 seconds Wall Sit (back against wall, legs 90 degrees)

C. Ab Circuit—3 rounds

- 8 Flutter Kick (L+R= 1 rep)

- 8 Hollow Rocks

- 8 Russian Twist (opt w/DB)

D. Finisher

5-Minute Plank (Switch every minute):

- 1 minute Forward Plank (forearms on ground)

- 1 minute Left Side Plank

- 1 minute Forward Plank

- 1 minute Right Side Plank

- 1 minute Forward Plank (alternate forearms to push-up plank, R or L arm/leg lift)

Workout #3

Warm-up

A. Tennis Ball Circuit

Take 12 tennis balls. With a black marker, write an exercise on each tennis ball. Put the balls in a bucket and place the bucket about 100-150m away. Class begins by doing a random exercise while the first class member runs to the bucket, grabs a tennis ball and brings it back to the class. The class then performs that exercise while the next class member runs to get the next tennis ball. Circuit is up when all 12 balls have been retrieved. When the last ball is brought to class, the instructor runs to retrieve the empty bucket while the class performs the final exercise. (You may use 24 tennis balls to make the circuit longer, repeat the exercises on the 12 additional balls.) Exercises I have used for the tennis balls are as follows:

- Jumping Jacks

- Burpees

- Airsquats

- Mountain Climbers

- Tuck Jumps

- Sit-ups

- High Knees

- Lunges (forward, reverse, or Jumping Lunges)

- Four Square Jump

- Squat Jumps

- Scissor Hops

- Plank Jacks

B. Stations:

Each member will set up the following equipment station for themselves in close proximity to a spot on the wall: a pair of dumbbells, a bodypump or Versa bar, a resistance band, and a cardio or plyo box. Each station is comprised of a 30-second movement using the specified piece of equipment. Once class finishes round one, rest 30 seconds and start round two. Perform each round two or three times, depending on time availability.

Round #1: 30 Seconds each movement

- DB: Curls

- BB or Versa Bar: Front Loaded Reverse Lunge

- ISO Hold: Wall Sit

- Band: Lateral Side Step

- Step/Box: Plyo Side Jump

- Rest: 30 Seconds

Round #2: 30 Seconds Each Movement

- DB: Press

- BB or Versa Bar: Back Squat

- ISO Hold: Plank

- Band: Pull Aparts

- Step/Box: Box Jump

- Rest: 30 Seconds

C. Ten 50-100m sprints

Start easy with each sprint progressively faster, and with a short recovery between each.

Workout #4

Warm-up

A. Circuits

Circuit #1 (1 minute each exercise, switch exercises as quickly as possible)

- Lateral Triplet (Dumbbell Lateral raise, Dumbbell front raise, bent over dumbbell lateral raise):

- Burpees

- Lateral Triplet

- Burpees

- Wall Sit

- Airsquats

- Planks

Rest 2 minutes

Circuit #2 (1 minute each except Mountain Climbers)

- Press

- Dumbbell or Kettlebell Goblet Squat

- Press

- Goblet Squat

- Mountain Climbers—2 minutes

- Hollow Rocks

Rest 2 minutes

Circuit #3 (1 minute each except Jacks)

- Push-ups

- Lunge Hold Right

- Push-ups

- Lunge Hold Left

- Jumping Jacks—2 minutes

- Sit-ups

B. Walk/Jog/Sprint

The following is to be done on a track or in similar circular space. Jog along with the class or get in the middle of the track with stopwatch, yell out the change in movements.

- 30/20/10 intervals

- 30 seconds Walk

- 20 seconds Jog

* 10 seconds Sprint as fast as possible

Repeat for a total of six rounds.

<u>Workout #5</u>

Warm-up

A. Leg Crusher—5 rounds

Round 1:

* 5 Squat Jumps

* 10 Mountain Climbers

* 10 Jumping Lunges

* 200m Run

Round 2

* 4 Squat Jumps

* 8 Mountain Climbers

    8 Jumping Lunges

* 200m Run

Round 3

* 3 Squat Jumps

- 6 Mountain Climbers

- 6 Jumping Lunges

- 200m Run

Round 4

- 2 Squat Jumps

- 4 Mountain Climbers

- 4 Jumping Lunges

- 200m Run

Round 5

- 1 Squat Jumps

- 2 Mountain Climbers

- 2 Jumping Lunges

- 200m Run

Rest 5 minutes and then repeat, but in reverse order of reps.

Round 1

- 1 Squat Jumps

- 2 Mountain Climbers

- 2 Jumping Lunges
- 200m Run

Round 2

- 2 Squat Jumps
- 4 Mountain Climbers
- 4 Jumping Lunges
- 200m Run

Round 3

- 3 Squat Jumps
- 6 Mountain Climbers
- 6 Jumping Lunges
- 200m Run

Round 4

- 4 Squat Jumps
- 8 Mountain Climbers
- 8 Jumping Lunges
- 200m Run

Round 5

- 5 Squat Jumps

- 10 Mountain Climbers

- 10 Jumping Lunges

- 200m Run

B. Dumbbell Complex—3 rounds, increase weight each round (start light!)

- 8 Cleans

- 8 Push Press

- 8 Monkey Jumps

- 8 Renegade Rows

C. Finisher

Tabata Airsquats (20 seconds work/10 seconds rest; repeat for a total of eight rounds)

Workout #6

Warm-up

A. 15/12/9/6/3

(Perform 15 reps of each movement in succession. Then go back and perform 12 reps of each movement in succession, etc)

- Barbell Front Squat or Heavy Goblet Squat

- Push-ups

- Supermans

Round #1: Tabatas

- Abs

- Side Plank Gravediggers

- Russian Twist

- Plank w/Tap

- Sit-ups

- Cardio

- DB Snatch

- Medball Slams

- Burpees

- Squat Jumps

Tabata #1/Abs: switch movement every 20 second intervals, so you will eventually do each exercise twice

Tabata #2/Cardio: switch movement every 20 second interval; do each exercise twice

Tabata #3: Abs: as above

Tabata #4: Cardio: as above

16 minutes total

Workout #7

Warm-up

A. Accumulator—1/1, 2/2, 3/3, 4/4, etc. (1 push-up, 1 weighted squat jump. 2 push-ups, 2 weighted squat jumps, etc. Continue for 5 minutes) 5 minutes each round

Round 1: 1/1, 2/2, 3/3, 4/4…

Push-ups

Weighted Squat Jumps

Rest 2 ½ minutes

Round 2: 1/1, 2/2, 3/3, 4/4….

Bicep Curls

Burpees

Rest 2 ½ minutes

Round 3: 1/1, 2/2, 3/3, 4/4...

DB Swing+Squat

Crunchy Frog

Rest 5 minutes; use this rest interval to set up bar/versa bar.

1 round Bear Complex (Bear Complex = Clean, Front Squat, Push Press, Back Squat, Push Press. This sequence = 1 rep. One round of Bear Complex = 7 reps):

- 200m Sprint

- Add weight to bar or take heavier Versa Bar

- 1 round Bear Complex

- 200m Sprint

- Add Weight

- 1 round Bear Complex

- 200m Sprint

- Add weight

- 1 round Bear Complex

- 200m Sprint

Workout #8

Warm-up

A. Tennis Ball Circuit (see Workout #3)

B. Strength Circuit

400m Run

10 Manmakers

20 Plank w/ Tap

30 DB Curls

40 Airsquats

400m Run

C. Tabatas—switch every 20-second interval

- Battle Ropes

- Ball Slams

- Scissor Hops

- Lateral Jumps

- Mountain Climbers

- Jumping Lunges

- Jumping Jacks

- Burpees

Workout #9

Warm-up

A. Obstacle Course

Each Round is 5 minutes in length

Round 1

- 10 Push-ups

- 50m Bear Crawl

- 10 Squat Jumps

- 150m Sprint

Rest 2 ½ minutes

Round 2

- 10 DB Press

- 50m Crab Walk

- 10 Jumping Lunges

- 150m Sprint

Rest 2 ½ minutes

Round 3

- 10 DB Renegade Rows

- 50m Prison Walk

- 10 180° Squat Jumps

- 150m Sprint

Rest 2 ½ minutes

Round 4

- 10 Airsquats

- 50m Burpee Broad Jump

- 10 Sit-ups

- 150m Sprint

Workout #10

Warm-up

A. Strength Accumu-Ladder

Write nine strength exercises on 8x11 cards

Exercise #1 is 30 seconds in duration, followed by 30 seconds rest

Add exercise #2 for 30 seconds, repeat exercise #1 for 30 seconds, 30 seconds rest

Exercise #3 for 30 seconds, repeat exercise #2 for 30 seconds, repeat exercise #1 30 seconds, 30 seconds rest, etc.

- Back Squat, Rest

- Read Loaded Forward Lunge, Back Squat, Rest

- Renegade Row, Rear Loaded Forward Lunge, Back Squat, Rest

- Bicep Curl, Renegade Row, Read Loaded Forward Lunge, Back Squat, Rest

- Front Squat, Bicep Curl, Renegade Row, Read Loaded Forward Lunge, Back Squat, Rest

- Front Loaded Reverse Lunge, Front Squat, Bicep Curl, Renegade Row, Read Loaded Forward Lunge, Back Squat, Rest

- Plank, Front Loaded Reverse Lunge, Front Squat, Bicep Curl, Renegade Row, Read Loaded Forward Lunge, Back Squat, Rest

- Thrusters, Plank, Front Loaded Reverse Lunge, Front Squat, Bicep Curl, Renegade Row, Read Loaded Forward Lunge, Back Squat, Rest

- Burpees, Thrusters, Plank, Front Loaded Reverse Lunge, Front Squat, Bicep Curl, Renegade Row, Read Loaded Forward Lunge, Back Squat

Workout #11

Warm-up

A. Dumbbell Complex: perform without releasing dumbbells until the end of the round.

- 10 Mountain Climbers (hands on dumbbells in the bottom position)

- 5 DB Squats

- 5 Lunges (each leg)

- 5 Curls

- 5 OH Presses

- 5 Renegade Rows

B. Cardio Complex

- 10 Burpees

- 9 Airsquats

- 8 Mountain Climbers (each leg)

- 7 Sit-ups

- 6 Jumping Lunges

- 5 Plank Jacks

- 4 Squat Jumps

- 3 Push-ups

- 2 Tuck Jumps

- 1 Plank Walkout

Rest 1 minute

Repeat DB Complex with increased weight

Repeat Cardio Complex

Rest 1 minute

Repeat DB Complex with increased weight

Repeat Cardio Complex

Workout #12

Warm-up

A. 3 x AMRAP 3 Rest 90 seconds between rounds

(Repeat 6 Push-ups and 6 DB curls for 3 minutes. Rest 90 seconds; repeat twice for a total of 3 rounds)

- 6 Push-ups

- 6 DB Curls

3 x AMRAP 3 Rest 90 seconds between rounds

(Repeat 6 Jumping Lunges and 6 Heavy Goblet Squats for 3 minutes. Rest 90 seconds; repeat twice for a total of 3 rounds)

- 6 Jumping Lunges

- 6 Heavy Goblet Squats

3 x AMRAP 3 Rest 90 seconds between rounds

(Repeat 6 Medball Slams and 6 Medball Sit-ups for 3 minutes. Rest 90 seconds; repeat twice for a total of 3 rounds)

- 6 Medball Slams

- 6 Sit-ups With Medball (ball touches behind head, then between feet)

B. Ab Buster

- 10 Rounds

- 10 second Plank

- 10 second Sit-ups

Workout #13

Warm-up

A. Bear Complex—3 rounds. Increase weight each round

(Bear Complex =Clean, Front Squat, Push Press, Back Squat, Push Press. This sequence =1 rep. One round of Bear Complex =7 reps).

B. 30's are wild

- 30 Push-ups

- 30 Lunges w/Plate OH

- Run 200m

- 30 DB Snatch

- 30 Burpees

- Run 400m

- 30 Squat Jumps

- 30 Box Jumps

- Run 800m

Workout #14

Warm-up

A. 5x10x10

(5 rounds, 10 exercises, 10 reps per exercise)

- Squat Jumps

- Push-ups

- Tuck Jumps

- Russian Twist

- Burpees

- Squat Cleans

- Mountain Climbers

- Thrusters

- Plank w/Shoulder Tap

- Weighted Lunges

B. Tabata Finisher: Change exercise every 20-second interval

- Burpees

- Scissor Kicks

- Push-ups

- Sit-ups

- Airsquats

- Fast Feet

- High Knees

- Tuck Jumps

Workout #15

Warm-up

A. Deck of Cards Cardio

Assign a specific exercise to each suit of cards. Perform the prescribed exercise the number of times designated by the number on the card. Go through the entire deck of cards.

Face Card = 10 reps of the exercise

Ace = 1 minute rest

Joker = 10 Burpees

Hearts = Airsquats

Diamonds = Mt. Climbers

Spades = Tuck Jumps

Clubs = Jumping Jacks

B. Glutapalooza

½ mile Run

then

2 Rounds

- 25 weighted Squat Jumps

- 25 Sit-ups

- 25 Goblet Squats

- 25 Supermans

Then

½ mile Run

Workout #16

Warm-up

A. Stations

Station #1

- 10 Push-ups

- 20 Sit-ups

- 40 Airsquats

- Repeat twice for a total of 3 rounds

Rest 3 minutes

Station #2

- 10 OH Press

- 20 Bicep Curls

- 40 Mountain Climbers

- Repeat twice for a total of 3 rounds

Rest 3 minutes

Station #3

- 10 Burpees

- 20 Goblet Squats

- 40 Jumping Jacks

- Repeat twice for a total of 3 rounds

Rest 3 minutes

Station #4

- 10 180-degree Squat Jumps

- 20 Box Jumps

- 40 Scissor Kicks

- Repeat twice for a total of 3 rounds

Workout #17

Warm-up

A. Leg Crusher

Ascending/Descending Ladder: 1/10, 2/9, 3/8, 4/7, 5/6, 6/5, 7/4, 8/3, 9/2, 10/1

Perform 1 weighted squat jump/10 jumping lunges. Then 2 weighted squat jumps/9 jumping lunges, etc. To help keep track as one progresses through the ladder, the total always equals 11.

Weighted Squat Jumps

Jumping Lunges (L+R=1)

150m Sprint

Rest two minutes, then ascend ladder

B. Arm/Shoulder Crusher

15 DB Press

30 DB Snatch (15L/15R)

15 Push-ups

10 Press

20 DB Snatch (10L/10R)

10 Push-ups

5 Press

10 DB Snatch (5L/5R)

5 Push-ups

Workout #18

Warm-ups

A. Descending Ladder Killer

10/9/8/7/6/5/4/3/2/1

- Tuck Jumps

- Airsquats

- Sit-ups

B. 4 Rounds

10 Jumping Lunges (L+R=1)

10 Push-ups

10 V-Ups

C. AMRAP 5

5 Thrusters

5 Burpees

50 Walking Lunges

Rest 2 minutes

REPEAT

<u>Workout #19</u>

Warm-up

A. 30 seconds on/30 seconds off

Airsquats

Forward/Reverse Lunges

Supermans

Hollow Rocks

Mountain Climbers

Jumping Jacks

Burpees

Tuck Jumps

B. DB Madness

- 30 DB Snatches (15L/15R)

- 30 Jumping Jacks

- 30 DB Thrusters

- 30 Jumping Jacks

- 30 DB Steps ups

- 30 Jumping Jacks

- 30 Renegade Rows

- 30 Jumping Jacks

- 30 Weighted Sit-ups

- 30 Jumping Jacks

- 30 Goblet Squats

- 30 Jumping Jacks

C. Sprint Finisher

10/100's (10 100m Sprints)

Workout #20

Warm-up

A. Strength Ladder Workout.

Perform each movement the designated number of reps. Rest only about 10 seconds before moving to the next number up the ladder (Example: 5 Push-ups/rest. 6 Push-ups/rest. 7 Push-ups/rest. etc. Then move to the next movement.)

5/6/7/8/9/10

Movements are as follows: Push-ups, Goblet Squat, DB Bicep Curl, DB Press, and Burpees.

B. 1/3/5/3/1 Circuit AMRAP

- 10 Lateral Hop Over Step/Box

- 10 Sit-ups

- 10 Squat Jumps

- 1 minute on/1 minute rest

- 10 Lateral Hop Over Step/Box

- 10 Sit-ups

- 10 Squat Jumps

- 3 minutes on/1 minute rest

- 10 Lateral Hop Over Step/Box

- 10 Sit-ups

- 10 Squat Jumps

- 5 minutes on/1 minute Rest

- 10 Lateral Hop Over Step/Box

- 10 Sit-ups

- 10 Squat Jumps

- 3 minutes on/1 minute rest

- 10 Lateral Hop Over Step/Box

- 10 Sit-ups

- 10 Squat Jumps

- 1 minute on/1 minute rest

Workout #21

Warm-up

A. 4 Rounds of Bear Complex—increase weight each round.

(Bear Complex = Clean, Front Squat, Push Press, Back Squat, Push Press. This sequence = 1 rep. One round of Bear Complex = 7 reps).

B.

10 Push-ups

10 Lunges with Plate OH

200m Run

10 DB Snatch (5L/5R)

10 Burpees

200m Run

10 Squat Jumps

10 Lateral Jumps

200m Run

Workout #22

Warm-up

A. Deck of Cards/Strength.

Assign a specific exercise to each suit of cards. Perform the prescribed exercise the number of times designated by the number on the card. Go through the entire deck of cards.

Face Card = 10 reps of the exercise

Ace = 1 minute Rest

Joker = 1 minute Plank

Hearts = Push-ups

Diamonds = Jumping Lunges

Spades = DB Bicep Curls

Clubs = Crunchy Frog

B. 25/20/15/10/5 Circuit

25 Sit-ups or Weighted Sit-ups

25 Squat Jacks

25 Renegade Rows (can go lighter DB for higher reps, heavier for lower reps)

Rest 1 minute

20 Sit-ups or Weighted Sit-ups

20 Squat Jacks

20 Renegade Rows

Rest 45 seconds

15 Sit-ups or Weighted Sit-ups

15 Squat Jacks

15 Renegade Rows

Rest 30 seconds

10 Sit-ups or Weighted Sit-ups

10 Squat Jacks

10 Renegade Rows

Rest 15 seconds

5 Sit-ups or Weighted Sit-ups

5 Squat Jacks

5 Renegade Rows

Workout #23

Warm-up

A. Perform the following together as a class:

5 rounds

- 15 Weighted Squat Jumps
- 30 second Squat Hold
- 30 seconds rest

Rest 2 minutes

5 rounds

- 15 Weighted Sit-ups
- 30 seconds V Hold
- 30 seconds rest

Rest 2 minutes

5 rounds

- 15 Bicep Curls
- 30 seconds Bicep Hold
- 30 seconds rest

B. Finisher

- 30 Jumping Jacks

- 20 Airsquats

- 10 Burpees

- 5 Plank Walkouts

- 10 Burpees

- 20 Airsquats

- 30 Jumping Jacks

Workout #24

Warm-up

A. Tabata Warm-up (20 seconds exercise, 10 seconds rest)

- Feet to Hand

- Inchworms

- Lunges

- Airsquats

- High Knees

- Butt Kicks

- Mountain Climbers

- Tuck Jumps

B. Circuit Strength/Cardio

You will set up alternating Strength/Cardio stations in a large circle around the room.

Class members will start at either a strength station or a cardio station. (There may be more than one person at each station.) Each station is 30 seconds in duration.

After 30 seconds, quickly transition clockwise or counterclockwise to the next work/cardio station and the next 30-second interval starts. The round is over when class members get to their original starting position (5 minutes total). Each round has a different cardio movement assigned to it. There are three rounds total.

In Round 1, the cardio movement = Mountain Climbers

In Round 2, the cardio movement = Tuck jumps

In Round 3, the cardio movement = Airsquats

Work Stations:

- Battle Ropes

- Cardio

- Ball Slams

- Cardio

- Push-ups

- Cardio

- Thrusters

- Cardio

- Goblet Squats

- Cardio

Workout #25

Warm-up

A.

20 Burpees

20 Sit-ups

20 Push-ups

20 Squat Jumps

40 Walking Lunges

2 Minute Plank

Rest 2 minutes

10 Burpees

10 Sit-ups

10 Push-ups

10 Squat Jumps

20 Walking Lunges

2 minute Plank

Rest 2 minutes

5 Burpees

5 Sit-ups

5 Push-ups

5 Squat Jumps

10 Walking Lunges

2 Minute Plank

B. 3 Rounds

- 30 seconds Jump the Line

- 30 seconds Mountain Climbers

- 30 seconds Scissor Kicks

- 30 seconds Plank Jacks

- 30 seconds Rest

Workout #26

Warm-up

A. This workout uses Barbells, Bodypumps bars, or Versa bars. There are 3 sets total. For each set, class members will use the same weight for their back squat, front squat, and row. For each successive set, add weight to the bar, but reduce the number of reps and the rest period.

20 Back Squats

20 Push-ups

200m Run

Rest 2 minutes

20 Front Squats

20 Burpees

200m Run

Rest 2 minutes

20 Rows

40 Walking Lunges

200m Run

Rest 2 minutes

ADD WEIGHT

10 Back Squats

10 Push-ups

100m Run

Rest 1 minute

10 Front Squats

10 Burpees

100m Run

Rest 1 minute

10 Rows

20 Walking Lunges

100m Run

Rest 1 minute

ADD WEIGHT

5 Back Squats

5 Push-ups

50m Run

Rest 30 seconds

5 Front Squats

5 Burpees

50m Run

Rest 30 seconds

5 Rows

10 Walking Lunges

50m Run

Workout #27

Warm-up

A. Manmakers/ISO Holds

5 Manmakers

- 15 seconds Split Squat Hold Right (keep the back knee just off the ground)

- 15 seconds Split Squat Hold Left (keep the back knee just off the ground)

- 15 seconds Push-up Hold (hold as close to bottom as possible without body touching the floor)

- 15 seconds V Hold

5 Manmakers

Repeat the isometric holds for 20 seconds

5 Manmakers

Repeat the isometric holds for 30 seconds

B. Cardio Ladder, for time (Repeat 2x)

- 10 Burpees

- 9 Airsquats

- 8 Mountain Climbers (L+R=1)

- 7 Sit-ups

- 6 Jumping Lunges

- 5 Plank Jacks

- 4 Squat Jumps

- 3 Push-ups

- 2 Tuck Jumps

- 1 Plank Walkout

- Rest 1 minute (each person times their own rest interval)

Workout #28

Warm-up

A. Tennis Ball Tabatas

(Use 24 tennis balls, you will have enough balls for 3 rounds of Tabatas)

- Tabata (Pick a new tennis ball each 20 second interval)

- 1 minute Front Plank

- Tabata (Pick a new tennis ball each 20 second interval)

- 1 minute Side Plank

- Tabata (Pick a new tennis ball each 20 second interval)

- 1 minute Side Plank

B. Dumbbell 8s

(perform together as class)

As many rounds as time allows, increase weight each round:

- 8 DB Squats

- 8 DB Hammer Curls

- 8 DB OH Presses

- 8 DB Snatches (4L/4R)

- 8 Renegade Rows

Workout #29

Warm-up

A. OTM

(At the top of every minute, perform the prescribed movement, and then perform the prescribed cardio movement for the remainder of the minute):

On Minute 1: 1 Manmaker/Jumping Jacks remainder of minute

On Minute 2: 2 Renegade Rows/High Knees remainder of minute

On Minute 3: 3 DB Thruster/Fast Feet remainder of minute

On Minute 4: 4 Burpees/Mountain Climbers remainder of minute

On minute 5: 3 DB Thrusters/Fast Feet remainder of minute

On Minute 6: 2 Renegade Row/High Knees remainder of minute

On Minute 7: 1 Manmaker/Jumping Jacks remainder of minute

B. 21/18/15/12/9/6/3

- Weighted Squat Jumps

- Push-ups

- Lateral Jump Over Box (Over and back = 1 rep)

C. AMRAP—5 minutes

(Perform 5 thrusters, 5 Burpees over the Bar, 50 walking lunges for 5 minutes. Rest 2 ½ minutes; repeat.)

- 5 Thrusters

- 5 Burpees Over the Bar

- 50 Walking Lunges

Rest 2 ½ minutes

Repeat AMRAP 5

Workout #30

Warm-up

A. Stations

- **Exercise A:** 60 seconds/Rest 30

- **Exercise B:** 30 seconds/Rest 30 (change stations)

Repeat the entire Circuit twice

Station #1

A. DB Goblet Squats

B. Push-ups

Station #2

A. DB Rows

B. Band Pull Aparts

Station #3

A. DB Curls

B. Mountain Climbers

Station #4

A. Plank Up/Downs

B. Tuck Jumps

B. 21's:

Call on each class member. Each picks their favorite movement; entire class performs 21 reps of that movement. Try not to repeat movements. Keep it moving quickly from member to member with as little rest as possible between.

C. Finisher

30/20/10 Walk/Jog/Sprint

6 Rounds

Workout #31

Warm-up

A. 5 Rounds

Every 3 minutes:

- Run 200m

- 9 DB Thrusters

- 9 Push-ups

- Rest remainder of 3 minutes. If you bump over the 3 min threshold, then adjust reps down to 6 so you have a little bit of rest.

B. 1-arm DB complex—Perform as a class:

- 6 reps per movement

- Snatch

- Clean and Press

- Drop Lunge

- Row

- Swing

- Drop the DB

- 50m Walking Lunges

- Repeat complex using the opposite arm.

Workout #32

Warm-up

A. 4 Rounds

- 6 reps of Bear Complex

- 9 Burpees

- 12 Weighted Sit-ups

- 16 Mountain Climbers

- 1 minute Plank Hold

- 200m sprint + 200m walk recovery

B. 15 second Cardio + Strength movement

(Perform the indicated cardio movement for 15 seconds, and then call out "Push-up." Class drops to the floor and performs one Push-up, and then jumps immediately up. Start the15 second cardio again, then Push-up. Do that for one full minute).

Jumping Jacks 15 seconds/1 Push-up x 4

Rest 1 minute

Mountain Climbers 15 seconds/1 Burpee x 4

C. 5 Minute Plank

- 1 minute Front Plank

- 1 minute Right Plank

- 1 minute Front Plank

- 1 minute Left Plank

- 1 minute Front Plank

Workout #33

Warm-up

A. 2 rounds

- 50 Jumping Jacks

- 10 Push-ups

- 10 Sit-ups

B. Tabata—1 round, change exercise each 20 second interval

- High Knees

- Butt Kicks

- Fast Feet

- Lateral Jumps

- Airsquats

- Four Corner Jump

- Mountain Climbers

- Tuck Jumps

C. 4 Rounds

Round 1

- 5 Push-ups

- 5 Weighted Squat Jumps

- 5 Plank w/Shoulder Tap

- 5 Burpees

- 50m Walking Lunges

Round 2

- 10 Push-ups

- 10 Weighted Squat Jumps

- 10 Plank w/Shoulder Tap

- 10 Burpees

- 50m Walking Lunges

Round 3

- 15 Push-ups

- 15 Weighted Squat Jumps

- 15 Plank w/Shoulder Tap

- 15 Burpees

- 50m Walking Lunges

Round 4

- 20 Push-ups

- 20 Weighted Squat Jumps

- 20 Plank w/Shoulder Tap

- 20 Burpees

- 50m Walking Lunges

<u>Workout #34</u>

Warm-up

A. 1 minute max reps (tell them to count their reps)

1 minute max Push-ups

Take 1 minute, go around class, and ask them how many reps they performed

1 minute max Airsquats

Take 1 minute, go around class, and ask them how many reps they performed

Then...

- 30 Mountain Climbers

- 5 Push-ups

- 25 Jacks

- 5 Burpees

- 20 High Knees

- 5 Squat Jumps

- 15 Sit-ups

- 5 Push-ups

- 10 Tuck Jumps

- 5 Burpees

- 10 Tuck Jumps

- 5 Push-ups

- 15 Sit-ups

- 5 Squat Jumps

- 20 High Knees

- 5 Burpees

- 25 Jacks

- 5 Push-ups

- 30 Mountain Climbers

B. 1 minute max reps (report on reps as above)

- Push-ups

- Airsquats

Then

- 400m Run

- 10 Manmakers

- 20 Plank with Shoulder Tap

- 30 DB Curls

- 40 Jumping Jacks

C. 1 minute max reps (report reps as above)

- Push-ups

- Airsquats

Workout #35

Warm-up

A. Four 4-minute AMRAPS, 2 minutes rest between rounds

AMRAP 4

- 10 DB Forward or Reverse Lunges

- 10 Sit-ups

- 10 Box Jumps

Rest 2 minutes

AMRAP 4

- 10 Burpees

- 10 DB Goblet Squats

- 10 Band Pull Aparts

Rest 2 minutes

AMRAP 4

- 10 DB Rows

- 10 Push-ups

- 10 Weighted Squat Jumps

Rest 2 minutes

AMRAP 4

- 10 Bicep Curls

- 10 Tricep Extensions

- 10 DB Presses

B. Isometric Holds—3 rounds

1st round: 15 second hold each movement

2nd round: 20 second hold each movement

3rd round: 30 second hold each movement

- Split Squat Right (keep back knee just off the ground)

- Split Squat Left (keep back knee just off the ground)

- Hollow Rock Hold

- Feet Elevated Push-up Hold (hold as close to the bottom as possible)

<u>Workout #36</u>

Warm-up

A. 21/15/9 Challenge

21/15/9

- Lateral Box Jumps

- Tuck Jumps

Rest 2 minutes

21/15/9

- Bent Over DB Rows

- Push-ups

Rest 2 minutes

21/15/9

- Squat Jumps

- Mountain Climbers

Rest 2 minutes

21/15/9

- Thrusters

- Burpees Over Bar

<u>Workout #37</u>

Warm-up

A. Cardio Accumu-Ladder

- 10 Jumping Jacks

- 10 Jumping Jacks, 10 Airsquats

- 10 Jumping Jacks, 10 Airsquats, 10 Mountain Climbers

- 10 Jacks, 10 Airsquats, 10 Mountain Climbers, 10 Lunges (L+R=1)

- 10 Jacks, 10 Airsquats, 10 Mountain Climbers, 10 Lunges, 10 Burpees

- 10 Jacks, 10 Airsquats, 10 Mountain Climbers, 10 Lunges, 10 Burpees, 10 Plank Jacks

- 10 Jacks, 10 Airsquats, 10 Mountain Climbers, 10 Lunges, 10 Burpees, 10 Plank Jacks, 10 Squat Jumps

- 10 Jacks, 10 Airsquats, 10 Mountain Climbers, 10 Lunges, 10 Burpees, 10 Plank Jacks, 10 Squat Jumps, 10 Push-ups

- 10 Jacks, 10 Airsquats, 10 Mountain Climbers, 10 Lunges, 10 Burpees, 10 Plank Jacks, 10 Squat Jumps, 10 Push-ups, 10 Tuck Jumps

- 10 Jacks, 10 Airsquats, 10 Mountain Climbers, 10 Lunges, 10 Burpees, 10 Plank Jacks, 10 Squat Jumps, 10 Push-ups, 10 Tuck Jumps, 10 Box Jumps

Workout #38

Warm-up

A. 3 rounds

- 20 Jumping Jacks

- 15 Airsquats

- 10 Sit-ups

- 5 Push-ups

- Run 200 meters

B. OTM (On the minute—probably end up about 4-5 minutes)

- 1 Manmaker/Jacks in remainder of the minute

- 2 Manmakers/Jacks

- 3 Manmakers/Jacks

- Etc. until failure

C. Chipper

- 100 Jumping Jacks

- 90 Airsquats

- 80 Mountain Climbers

- 70 Sit-ups

- 60 Plank Jacks

- 50 Box Jumps

- 40 Tuck Jumps

- 30 Push-ups

- 20 Squat Jumps

- 10 Burpees Over Box

<u>Workout #39</u>

Warm-up

A.

50 Push-ups (scale to knees if necessary)

50 Airsquats

50 Crunchy Frog or Sit-ups

50 Jumping Jacks

B.

21 DB Thrusters

21 Burpees

400m Run

15 DB Thrusters

15 Burpees

15 DB Push Press

400m Run

9 DB Thrusters

9 Burpees

9 DB Push Press

9 Renegade Rows

400m Run

Workout #40

Warm-up

A. Box Jump for height.

Teams of three. Use steps, build in height. Two members stand at each end of step to make sure it stays stable as team member jumps.

B. Farmer Carry Races

- Pace off a 150m lap.

- Each class member will have a turn running/walking as fast as possible carrying a weighted plate or heavy dumbbell in each hand. (Plates are easier to run with.) Time the lap for each individual and record that time.

- Male: 45lb plate in each hand

- Female: 25lb plate in each hand

- If time allows, repeat so everyone gets two attempts.

C. Tabata Finisher:

Change exercise each 20-second interval. Two rounds, rest 1 minute between rounds:

- Sit-ups

- Tuck Jumps

- Mountain Climbers

- Plank Up/Downs

- Airsquats

- Push-ups

- Jumping Jacks

- Squat Jumps

Workout #41

Warm-up

A. Three rounds total; increase weight each round:

- 16 Front Loaded (BB) or DB Reverse Lunges (8 each leg)

- Rest 1 minute

- 1 minute Plank

- Rest 1 minute

B. Dumbbell Complex—Three Rounds Total

- 10 Mountain Climbers

- 10 Squats

- 10 Lunges

- 10 Bicep Curls

- 10 Press

- 10 Renegade Rows

- Rest 2 minutes

Workout #42

Warm-up

A. AMRAP Circuit

1 minute Mountain Climbers

Rest 1 minute

4 minute AMRAP

- 10 Weighted Lunges (L+R=1)
- 10 Burpees

Rest 1 minute

4 minute AMRAP

- 10 HRPU (Hand Release Push Ups)
- 10 Burpees

Rest 1 minute

4 minute AMRAP

- 10 Box Jumps
- 10 Burpees

Rest 1 minute

1 minute Mountain Climbers

B. Finisher

10/9/8/7/6/5/4/3/2/1

- Squat Jacks

- Tuck Jumps

Workout #43

Warm-up

A. 20/15/10/5 with run after each round

Round 1:

- 20 Push-ups

- 20 Russian Twists

- 20 Box Kickovers

- 20 Tricep Dips on box or step

- 20 Weighted Squat Jumps

- 20 Lateral Box Jumps

- 20 Medball Slams

- 20 Burpees

Run 50 meters

Round 2:

- 15 Push-ups

- 15 Russian Twists

- 15 Box Kickovers

- 15 Tricep Dips on box or step

- 15 Weighted Squat Jumps (increase weight from previous round)

- 15 Lateral Box Jumps

- 15 Medball Slams

- 15 Burpees

Run 100 meters

Round 3:

- 10 Push-ups

- 10 Russian Twists

- 10 Box Kickovers

- 10 Tricep Dips on box or step

- 10 Weighted Squat Jumps (increase weight from previous round)

- 10 Lateral Box Jumps

- 10 Medball Slams

- 10 Burpees

Run 200 meters

Round 4:

- 5 Push-ups

- 5 Russian Twists

- 5 Box Kickovers

- 5 Tricep Dips on box or step

- 5 Weighted Squat Jumps (increase weight from previous round)

- 5 Lateral Box Jumps

- 5 Medball Slams

- 5 Burpees

Run 400 meters

<u>Workout #44</u>

Warm-up

A. OTM (on the minute) until failure

- Burpees

- Airsquats

- Mountain Climbers

Explanation:

At the top of the first minute, perform 1 Burpee, 1 Airsquat, 1 Mt. Climber (L+R=1)

At the top of second minute, 2 Burpees, 2 Airsquats, 2 Mt Climbers (L+R=1)

At the top of third minute, 3 Burpees, 3 Airsquats, 3 Mt Climbers (L+R=1)

Repeat until you cannot finish the assigned number of reps within the minute.

Once you reach failure, perform a plank until remaining class members finish to failure.

B. Circuits:

Perform each round three times. Rest as a class between rounds, 5 minutes between rounds.

Round 1

- 20 Russian Twists

- 20 Plank w/Shoulder Tap

- 20 Sit-ups

Repeat twice

Rest 5 minutes

Round 2

- 15 Bicep Curls

- 15 OH Presses

- 15 Bent Over Rows

Repeat twice

Rest 5 minutes

Round 3

- 50 Mountain Climbers

- 50 Airsquats

- 50 Lunges (25L, 25R)

Repeat twice

Workout #45

Warm-up

A. RUN + TABATAS

Run 200 meters (Wait until all class members return)

Tabata Front Squats (Barbell)

Rest 1 minute

Run 200 meters

Tabata Mountain Climbers/Tuck Jumps

Rest 1 minute

Run 200 meters

Tabata Burpees

Rest 1 minute

Run 200 meters

Tabata Jump Lunges or Squat Jumps

Rest 1 minute

Run 200 meters

Tabata Back Squats (Barbell or versa bar)

Workout #46

Warm-up

A. 10 rounds

- 10 seconds Sit-ups

- 10 seconds Plank

B.

For time: Class members record their time for each round. Rest 5 minutes between rounds. If time allows, repeat each round after the 5-minute rest period and try to beat previous time.

Round 1

- 50 Jacks

- 40 Airsquats

- 30 Lateral Jumps

- 20 Burpees

- 10 Thrusters

Rest 5 Minutes

Round 2

- 50 Box Jumps

- 40 Plank Jacks

- 30 Squat Jumps

- 20 Plank w/ Shoulder Tap

- 10 Push-ups

Rest 5 minutes

Round 3

- 50 Mountain Climbers

- 40 Sit-ups

- 30 Jumping Lunges

- 20 Jump Throughs

- 10 Tuck Jumps

Workout #47

Warm-up

A. Minute Madness

Perform each movement in succession for 1 minute; immediately move on to the next round after the 1-minute rest period.

Round 1

- Squat Cleans

- Burpees

- DB Snatches

- Push-ups

- Sit-ups

Rest 1 minute

Round 2

- Push Press

- Burpees

- DB Snatches

- HRPU

- Jump the Line

Rest 1 minute

Round 3

- DB Thrusters

- Burpees

- DB Snatches

- Renegade Rows

- Mountain Climbers

B. 30/20/10 Walk/Jog/Sprint x 6

<u>Workout #48</u>

Warm-up

A. OTM 10 (On the minute for 10 minutes)

- Even minutes: 150m Sprint

- Odd minutes: 15 heavy Weighted Squat Jumps

B. 10/1, 9/2, 8/3, 7/4, 6/5, 5/6,4/7, 3/8,2/9, 10/1

- Push-ups

- Airsquats

C.

8 Squat Cleans

16 Sit-ups

24 Burpees

16 Sit-ups

8 Squat Cleans

16 Sit-ups

24 Burpees

16 Sit-ups

8 Squat Cleans

Workout #49

Warm-up

A. 50/40/30/20/10 seconds

50 seconds each movement

- Squat Jumps

- Sit-ups

- Push-ups

- Lunges

- Burpees

Rest 1 Minute

40 seconds each movement

- Squat Jumps

- Sit-ups

- Push-ups

- Lunges

- Burpees

Rest 1 Minute

30 seconds each movement

- Squat Jumps

- Sit-ups

- Push-ups

- Lunges

- Burpees

Rest 1 minute

20 seconds each movement

- Squat Jumps

- Sit-ups

- Push-ups

- Lunges

- Burpees

Rest 1 minute

10 seconds each movement

- Squat Jumps

- Sit-ups

- Push-ups

- Lunges

- Burpees

B. Dumbbell 8's

As many rounds as time allows (try for 3) increase weight each round:

- 8 DB Squats

- 8 DB Hammer Curls

- 8 DB OH Press

- 8 DB Snatches (4L/4R)

- 8 Renegade Rows

<u>Workout #50</u>

Warm-up

A.

400m Run

12 Mountain Climbers

10 Tuck Jumps

8 DB Snatches

6 Weighted Squat Jumps

4 Manmakers

2 Burpees

Sprint 50m

Rest 2 minutes

Repeat

B. 10/8/6/4/2

(Perform 10 Burpees, then Walking Lunges/Sprint. Then 8 Burpees, Walking Lunges/Sprint; etc)

- Burpees

- 50m Walking Lunges

- 50m Sprint

Workout #51

Warm-up

A. 5/4/3/2/1

5 minutes total

- 1 minute Lateral Box Jumps

- 1 minute Box Jumps

- 1 minute Kickovers

- 1 minute Box Jumps

- 1 minute Lateral Box Jumps

4 minutes total

- 1 minute Jumping Jacks

- 1 minute Mountain Climbers

- 1 minute Jumping Jacks

- 1 minute Mountain Climbers

3 minute AMRAP

- 10 Push-ups

- 10 Sit-ups or Weighted Sit-ups

2 minutes

- 30 seconds Airsquats

- 30 seconds Squat Jumps

- 30 seconds Airsquats

- 30 seconds Squat Jumps

1 minute Plank

B. 3 Rounds

- 7 Front Squats

- 11 Burpees Over Bar

- 7 Front Squats

- Rest 90 seconds

Workout #52

Warm-up

A. OTM 10 (On the minute for 10 minutes)

- 3 Clapping Push-ups (modify to the knees if necessary)

- 5 Weighted Squat Jumps

At the top of each minute, perform 3 Clapping Push-ups and 5 Weighted Squat Jumps. Rest the remainder of the minute.

B.

400m Run

20 Goblet Squats

20 Push-ups

20 DB Presses

20 Bicep Curls

20 DB Split Squats (10R/10L)

20 Weighted Sit-ups

400m Run

CHAPTER 5: THEMED WORKOUTS

Partner Workouts: I use partner workouts to add variety to the workouts. They are fun, they keep spirits high, and they help members stay motivated and often boost their intensity, since it sparks friendly competition.

Partner Workout #1

Teams of 2—One person works while one rests. Before starting, discuss your strategy of distributing/partitioning reps. (e.g. each partner alternates doing 5 Burpees each before reaching 50; then alternates doing 10 Squat Jumps each until reaching 50; etc). Must complete all reps of the prescribed movement before moving on to next movement. Help your partner count the reps and cheer your partner on through their reps.

Run 400m together as a team (both must finish run before starting movements)

50 Burpees

50 Squat Jumps

50 Push-ups

50 Walking Lunges

50 DB Push Presses

50 Goblet Squats

50 Medball Slams

50 Plank with Shoulder Tap

Run 400m together

Partner Workout #2

Teams of 2—One performs the prescribed movement while the other holds the isometric exercise. Switch when partner 1 completes all 20 reps.

20 Squat Cleans/Squat Hold (hold squat at the bottom)

20 Sit-ups/Wallsit—legs at 90-degree angle

20 Thrusters/Plank Hold

20 Burpees/V-Sit Hold

Partner Workout #3

Burpeepalooza!

Teams of 2—One person works while one rests. Before starting, discuss your strategy of distributing/partitioning reps. (e.g. each partner alternates doing 5 Burpees each before reaching 10; then alternates doing 25 Mountain Climbers each until reaching 100; etc). Must complete all reps of the prescribed movement before moving on to next movement.

10 Burpees

100 Mountain Climbers

10 Burpees

100 Jumping Jacks

10 Burpees

100 Airsquats

10 Burpees

100 Lunges

10 Burpees

100 Tuck Jumps

10 Burpees

100 Plank Jacks

10 Burpees

100 Jump the Line

10 Burpees

Partner Workout #4

Teams of 2—One works while the other rests. Partner 1 performs 10 Thrusters while Partner 2 rests. Then Partner 2 performs 10 Thrusters while Partner 1 rests. Each person must complete all reps before moving on to the next movement. Continue for 5 minutes. Rest 2 ½ minutes and move on to the next AMRAP.

5 minute AMRAP

- 10 DB Thrusters (partners may use different weights if necessary)

- 10 Burpees

2 ½ minutes Rest

5 minute AMRAP

- 10 Sit-ups

- 10 Jumping Lunges

2 ½ minutes rest

5 minute AMRAP

- 10 Push-ups

- 10 DB Squat Cleans

2 ½ minutes rest

5 minute AMRAP

- 10 Medball Slams

- 10 Weighted Squat Jumps

Partner Workout #5

Medball Madness

Teams of 2—Each team has one medball. One works while the other rests. You may split up reps any way between the two, but must finish all reps before moving to the next movement.

Run 400m, passing medball back and forth while running

20 Medball Sit-up Throws to Partner

40 Walking Lunges with Medball Overhead

60 Medball Push-ups

80 Medball Squat Passes to Partner

100 Medball Slams

80 Medball Squat Passes to Partner

60 Medball Push-ups

40 Walking Lunges with Medball Overhead

20 Medball Sit-up Throws to Partner

Run 400m, passing Medball back and forth ¶

Partner Workout #6

Teams of 3: Each team forms a single file line, one behind each other, facing the front of class.

Explanation:

The person in the front of the line (Player A) runs 200 meters. While Player A runs:

- The next person in line (Player B) performs Push-ups

- The next person in line (Player C) performs Goblet Squats

When player A returns,

- He/she goes to the back of the line and performs Goblet Squats.

- Player B moves up and runs.

- Player C moves up and performs Push-ups.

When player B returns,

- They go to the back of the line and Goblet Squat

- Player C runs

- Player A moves up and does Push-ups

Continue for 5 minutes

3 minutes rest between rounds

Round 1

Player A: 200m Run

Player B: Push-ups

Player C: Goblet Squats

Round 2

Player A: 200m Run

Player B: Inchworms

Player C: Renegade Rows

Round 3

Player A: 200m Run

Player B: Plank Hold

Player C: DB Thrusters

Partner Workout #7

Domino Plank/Run Race

This is a quick fun finisher, contributing to a lot of team spirit. Split class into two teams. Have each team set up in a plank position facing a member of the opposite team.

At your command, teams raise up into a plank hold while the team members on one end get up and sprint a 50m down and back. Once the team runner returns, they fall into a plank position and the next team member jumps up to sprint the 50m down/back. Team finishing first wins.

Birthday Workouts: I like to recognize class members on their birthdays if possible. I find milestone birthdays to be especially appropriate for a tailored workout. Be creative using a rounds/rep scheme utilizing the date and year of their birthday, or take their age and perform that number of reps for a set of exercises.

Birthday Workout #1

Turning 30. Each round has 2 exercises, 3 sets per round. Sets are either 30 seconds or 30 reps.

Round 1—Squat Jumps & Push-ups

Set 1: 30 reps

Set 2: 30 seconds

Set 3: 30 reps

Example:

Set 1: Perform 30 Squat Jumps then 30 Push-ups

Set 2: 30 seconds of Squat Jumps then 30 seconds of Push-ups

Set 3: Perform 30 Squat Jumps then 30 Push-ups

Round 2—Tricep Dips (on step or box) & Box Jumps

Set 1: 30 reps

Set 2: 30 seconds

Set 3: 30 reps

Round 3—Mountain Climbers & Burpees

Set 1: 30 seconds

Set 2: 30 reps

Set 3: 30 seconds

Round 4—DB Rows & Bicep Curls

Set 1: 30 reps

Set 2: 30 seconds

Set 3: 30 reps

Round 5—Goblet Squats & Sit-ups

Set 1: 30 seconds

Set 2: 30 reps

Set 3: 30 seconds

Round 6—DB Front Raise & Lateral Raise

Set 1: 30 seconds

Set 2: 30 reps

Set 3: 30 seconds

Round 7—Hollow Rocks & Plank Up/Downs

Set 1: 30 reps

Set 2: 30 seconds

Set 3: 30 reps

Round 8—Jumping Jacks & Plank Jacks

Set 1: 30 seconds

Set 2: 30 reps

Set 3: 30 seconds

Round 9—Russian Twist & Supermans

Set 1: 30 reps

Set 2: 30 seconds

Set 3: 30 reps

Round 10—Jumping Lunges & Glute Bridges

Set 1: 30 reps

Set 2: 30 seconds

Set 3: 30 reps

<u>Birthday Workout #2</u>

Turning 40 on the 11th day of the month. 11 exercises, 40 reps each exercise. Must complete all 40 reps before moving on to next exercise.

- Weighted Sit-ups

- DB Thrusters

- Tuck Jumps

- DB Bicep Curls

- Push-ups

- DB Snatches

- DB Squat Cleans

- Russian Twists

- Box Jumps

- DB Tricep Extensions

- Squat Jumps

- Burpees

Holiday Workouts: Make the holidays special with these themed workouts. Add extra fun by dressing in holiday colors.

Christmas Workout #1

12 Days of Christmas: This format works exceptionally well for a workout. Rep scheme corresponds to the numeric scheme in the song "12 Days of Christmas." For example,

Perform 200m run. Then 2 Push Press, 200m run. Then 3 Squat Cleans, 2 Push Press, 200m run. Then 4 Tuck Jumps, 3 Squat Cleans, 2 Push Press, 200m Run, etc.

1 Two Hundred Meter Run

2 Push Presses

3 Squat Cleans

4 Tuck Jumps

5 Renegade Rows

6 Weighted Squat Jumps

7 Jumping Jacks

8 Barbell Thrusters

9 Weighted Sit-ups

10 Walking Lunges

11 Burpee Box Jumps

12 Mountain Climbers

Christmas Workout #2

Write the word "Christmas" vertically down a chalkboard/whiteboard, and then use each letter of the word Christmas as the first letter for a movement or exercise. Class then performs 25 reps of each movement or exercise.

Curls

Hand Release Push-ups

Rows w/ Resistance Band

Inchworms

Sit-ups

Thrusters w/DB

Mountain Climbers

Airsquats

Supermans

Valentine's Day Workout

Use the month, day of the month, and year as the structure for the workout.

(e.g. February 14, 2014 = 2/14/14)

Two Rounds, 14 exercises, 14 reps per exercise

- Airsquats

- Push-ups

- Jumping Lunges

- Plank w/ Shoulder Tap

- DB Thrusters

- Mountain Climbers

- Banded or DB Rows

- Lateral Box Jump

- Sit-ups

- Burpees

- Supermans

- DB Squat Cleans

- Box Jumps

- Tuck Jumps

Halloween Workout

10 Spooktacular Supermans

31 Jack O Lantern Jumping Jacks

10 Goblin Goblet Squats

31 Jack O Lantern Jumping Jacks

10 Bat Burpees

31 Jack O lantern Jumping Jacks

10 Great Pumpkin Push-ups

31 Jack O Lantern Jumping Jacks

10 Scary Squat Jumps

31 Jack O Lantern Jumping Jacks

10 Demon Dumbbell Curls

31 Jack O Lantern Jumping Jacks

10 Vampire V-ups

31 Jack O Lantern Jumping Jacks

10 Paces Frankenstein Walk

31 Jack O Lantern Jumping Jacks

10 Corpse Crunches

31 Jack O Lantern Jumping Jacks

10 steps Creepy Crab Crawl

31 Jack O Lantern Jumping Jacks

CHAPTER 6: GLOSSARY

Listed below is a detailed glossary of every single movement or exercise used in all of the workouts, in alphabetical order.

Airsquat (bodyweight squat): Stand with feet a little wider than hip width apart, toes turned out slightly and arms extended in front. Bend knees slowly, sit hips back and down behind as if sitting down into a chair. Keep the knees tracking over toes and weight balanced towards the heels.

AMRAP: As Many Reps as Possible/As Many Rounds As Possible. Complete a circuit as many times as possible within a given timeframe.

Arm Circles: Stand with feet hip width apart with arms raised at sides. Draw small forward circles with arms. Reverse direction.

Band Pull Aparts: Stand shoulder width apart. Grab a medium resistance band about 12 inches apart and hold directly in front of chest. Pull the band away from itself until the hands are in line with the body perpendicular from the body and parallel to the floor.

Barbell Back Squat: Stand with feet shoulder width apart and with toes pointed out slightly. Bar is placed behind head on shoulder blades. Sit the hips back, bend the knees and hips to lower the torso, and return to upright position.

Barbell Clean: Start with the barbell in an overhand grip with a bend at the knees, chest lifted and back and arms straight. Drive through the heels and explode up while shrugging the barbell up to receive it on shoulders.

Barbell Front Squat: Start with the barbell in the front rack position —the barbell rests on the collarbones, fingertips resting on the barbell, and elbows pointing straight ahead. Grip should be slightly wider than the shoulders and palms should be facing up. With feet hip width apart, lower down into a squat, then return to the start and repeat.

Barbell Press: Start with the barbell in the front rack position—the barbell rests on the collarbones, fingertips resting on the barbell, and elbows pointing straight ahead. Hold the barbell with hands slightly wider than shoulder width at the shoulders. Press the bar up until arms are extended overhead.

Barbell Push Press: Start with the barbell in the front rack position —the barbell rests on the collarbones, fingertips resting on the barbell, and elbows pointing straight ahead. Hold the barbell with hands slightly wider than shoulder width at the shoulders. Bend at the knees and then push up with the legs as you press the bar straight over the shoulders.

Barbell Rows: Stand with feet hip width apart, knees slightly bent and bar in an overhand grip. Bend at the waist and bend elbows and pull bar to the rib cage. Keep the back straight as you row.

Battle Ropes Waves: To start, stand facing the anchor with feet shoulder width apart. Grasp one end of the rope in each hand so that palms face each other. Bend knees slightly, brace your core, and move both arms up and down rapidly, creating big waves in the rope.

Bear Complex: A barbell movement comprised of the following movements: Clean, Front Squat, Push Press, Back Squat, and Push Press. Those movements equal one rep. Do not set the bar down between movements or reps. One round of Bear Complex equals 7 reps.

Bear Crawl: Drop onto all fours with hands directly under the shoulders, then raise up onto the feet. Move the right hand and left leg forward simultaneously. Then move the left hand and right leg forward. Repeat to bear crawl. Make sure the knees never touch the ground.

Bicep Curls: Stand with feet shoulder width apart. Hold dumbbells in both hands with palms up. Bend both elbows simultaneously bringing both dumbbells up to the chest, keeping elbows close to the sides.

Box Jump: Stand in front of a plyo box or cardio step. Jump onto box and immediately back down to same position. Immediately repeat. Jump back and forth from floor and box as fast as possible.

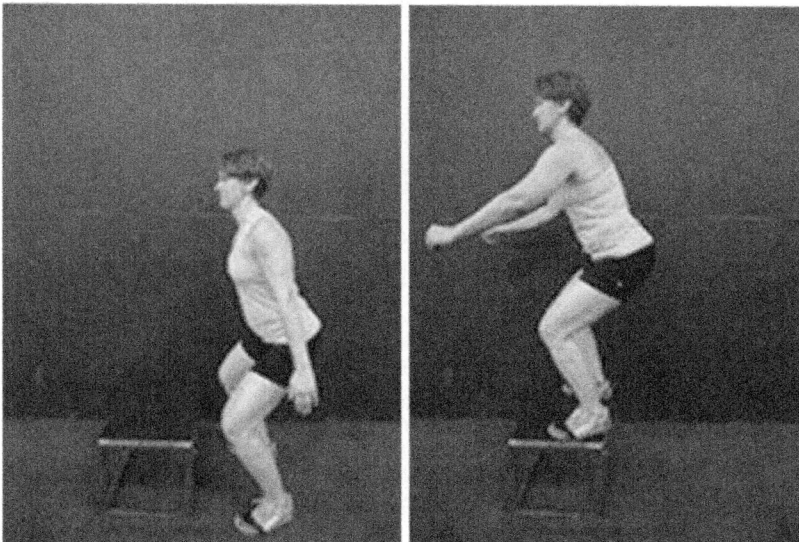

Box Kickover: Line up laterally with a cardio step. Put hands at top of cardio step. With hands planted on the step, jump laterally over the box onto the floor from side to side as fast as possible.

Burpees: Start in a standing position. Kick both feet back, while simultaneously lowering into the bottom portion of a push-up. Arms will not be extended. Immediately jump to feet to the squat position, while simultaneously pushing "up" with both arms. Leap up as high as possible from the squat position and clap overhead.

Burpee Broad Jump: Perform a burpee, instead of jumping and clapping overhead at the end of the movement, perform a squat jump forward. Land, and repeat the burpee.

Burpee Over Bar: Line up laterally to or facing a barbell. Perform a burpee, instead of a clap at the top, jump over the bar.

Butt Kicks: Stand tall on the balls of the feet, hip width apart. Rapidly kick one heel up to the butt, alternating legs. Go fast!

Carioca: Start in an athletic stance with feet hip width apart. Traverse while crossing one foot in front then behind the other. After a specified distance, switch directions.

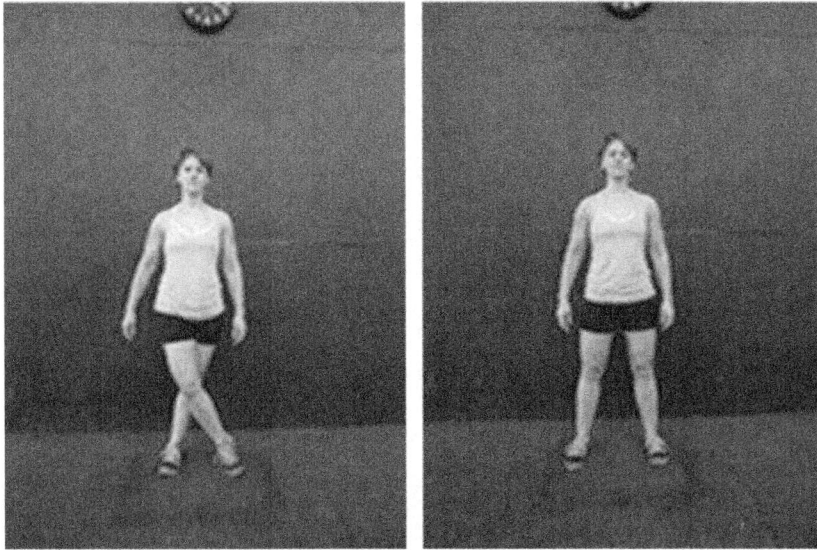

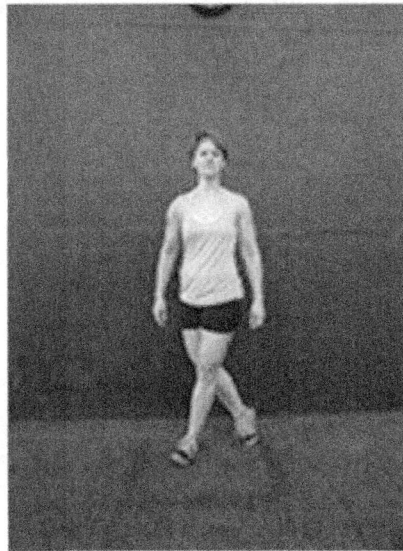

Crab Walk: Similar to a bear crawl, but facing upwards. Sit on the floor, and then lift up on the hands and feet. Crawl in each direction, like a crab.

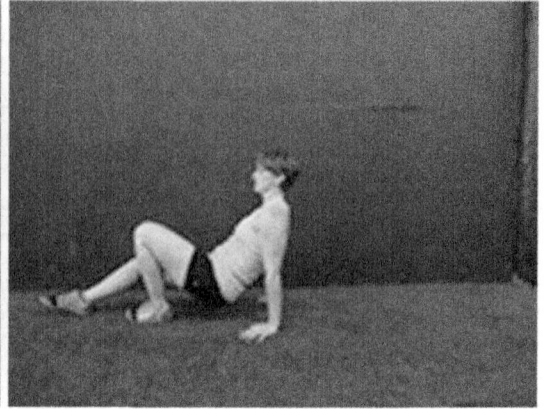

Crunchy Frog: In a V-like sitting position, wrap arms around the legs. Quickly open up by moving the arms out to the sides and extending the legs out in front. Bring them back in and repeat.

Dislocators (Pass Throughs): Start with feet shoulder width apart. PVC Pipe or resistance band at waist with a wide overhand grip. Keeping arms locked out, bring the PVC pipe overhead and down to the lower back until it touches butt, return to starting position and repeat.

Drop Lunge: Hold one dumbbell at the shoulder. Step backwards into a reverse lunge with the same side leg as the dumbbell is on. Drive back up to the start position and repeat.

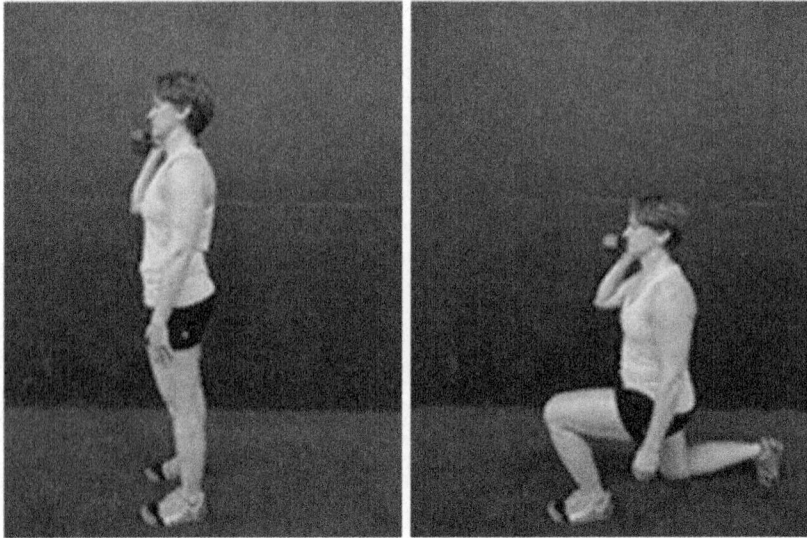

Dumbbell Bent Over Reverse Fly: Stand with feet hip width apart, knees slightly bent and dumbbells in neutral grip. Bend at the waist to a 45-degree angle. Raise your arms out to your sides, squeezing your shoulder blades together at the top for a second.

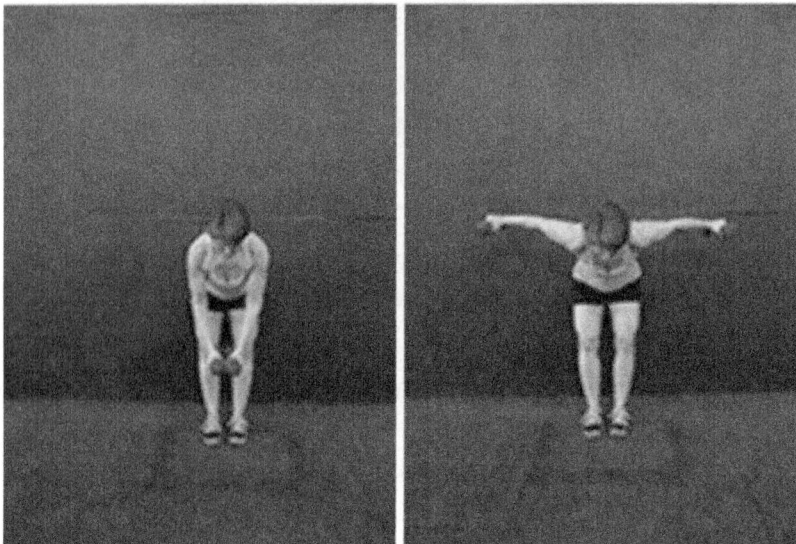

Dumbbell Clean: Stand with feet shoulder width apart in a partial squat position. Hold a pair of dumbbells at sides with palms facing each other. Drive through the heels and explode up while shrugging the dumbbells to receive them on shoulders. Lower the dumbbells to side and return to the starting position.

Dumbbell Curl: (See Bicep Curl)

Dumbbell Front Raise: Hold onto a pair of dumbbells in front of the upper thighs with elbows straight or slightly bent. Raise dumbbells forward and upward until the arms are just above horizontal. Lower and repeat.

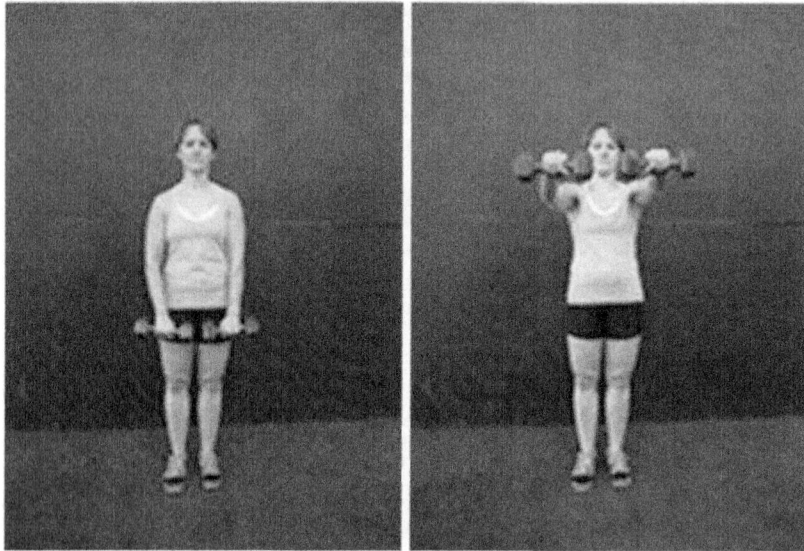

Dumbbell Lateral Raise: Stand with feet hip width apart, a pair of dumbbells in hands, palms facing the thighs. Lift arms out to the sides to shoulder level. Lower the dumbbells and repeat. Maintain a slight bend in the elbows to protect the joints.

Dumbbell Press: Stand with a pair of dumbbells. Raise the weights up to shoulders with palms facing the ears and elbows bent so they are directly underneath the weights. Push the dumbbells overhead until arms are fully extended. Lower the dumbbells back to the shoulders.

Dumbbell Push Press: Stand holding a pair of dumbbells with arms bent and palms facing each other. Bend at the knees and then push up with the legs as you press the weights straight over the shoulders. Lower the dumbbells back to the starting position and repeat.

Dumbbell Row: Stand with feet hip width apart, knees slightly bent and dumbbells in hand. Bend at the waist to a 45-degree angle. Draw the elbows back and pull the dumbbells to the rib cage. Lower and repeat.

Dumbbell Snatch: Using an overhand grip, grab a dumbbell in one hand and stand with the feet slightly wider than shoulder width apart. Descend hips to the floor until the knees are bent at 90 degrees and the dumbbell is resting on the floor. Quickly pull the dumbbell toward the ceiling while simultaneously extending the knees and hips and raising the body on the balls of the feet. Avoid swinging dumbbell away from the body. (The cue I use is zip up your jacket.) As the dumbbell reaches its highest point, quickly rotate the elbow under the weight and extend the arm. The dumbbell will rest over the top of the shoulder with the palm facing away from the body.

Dumbbell Squat Clean: Perform a dumbbell clean but land and receive the dumbbells in the bottom of a squat.

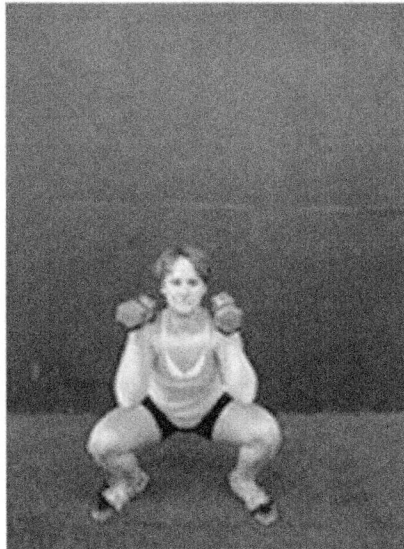

Dumbbell Step Ups: Use a bench or low step and set up height so that when one leg is on the step, that leg forms a 90-degree angle. With dumbbells in both hands, step up with one leg and bring trailing leg up to step. Return feet, one at a time, to the ground. Be conscious to press down through the lead foot and resist pushing off with the back foot.

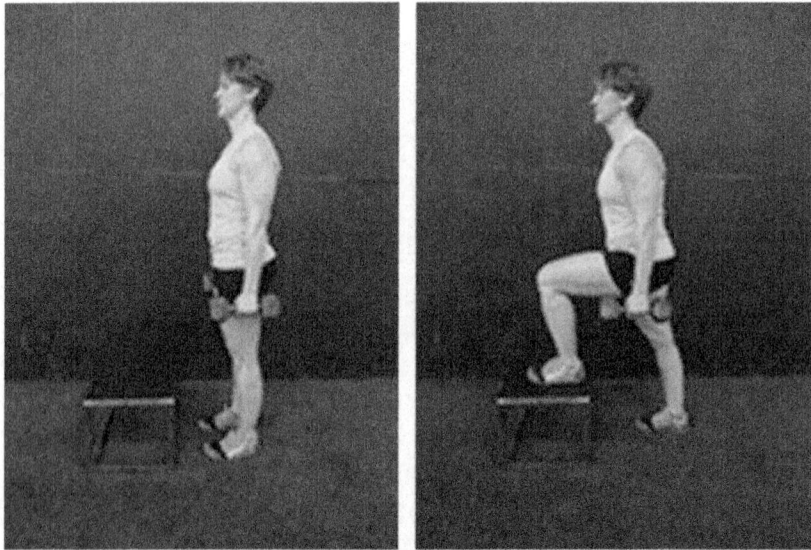

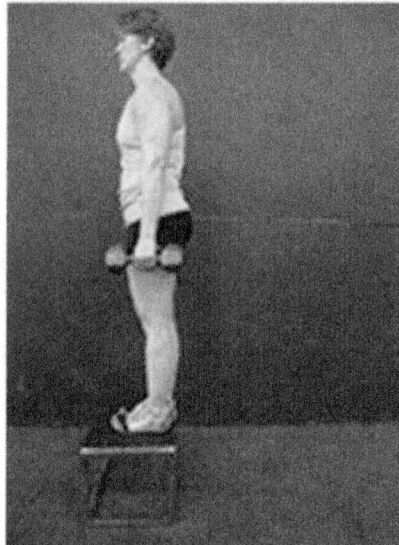

Dumbbell Swing + Squat: Stand tall with feet hip width apart. Hold a dumbbell vertically by the top knob, with arms extended and elbows unbent. Hinge forward at the hips, letting the dumbbell swing between your legs behind you. Thrust hips forward while swinging the dumbbell forward, at the apex of the swing, release the dumbbell and catch against the chest in the goblet position as you descend into a squat. Stand and repeat.

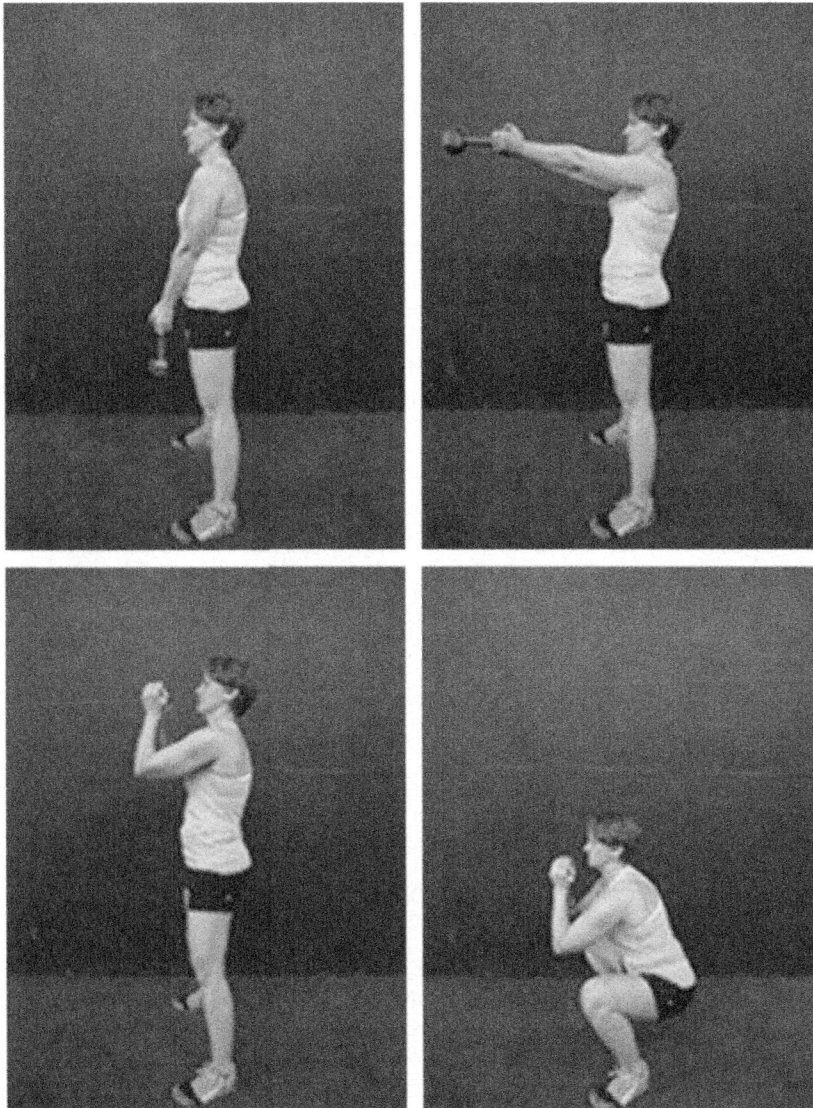

Dumbbell Thruster: Hold dumbbells at the shoulders with palms facing the ears. Drop into a full squat position while keeping the dumbbells at shoulder level. Return to standing position in an explosive (thrusting) motion and push the dumbbells up overhead.

Dumbbell Tricep Extension: Sit or stand holding a dumbbell with one or both hands. Extend the arms overhead, elbows next to ears.

Bend at the elbow to lower the weight behind the head and slowly back up. Be careful not to arch the back.

EMOM: Every Minute On the Minute

Farmer Carry: Pick up two heavy dumbbells or kettlebells and walk for distance.

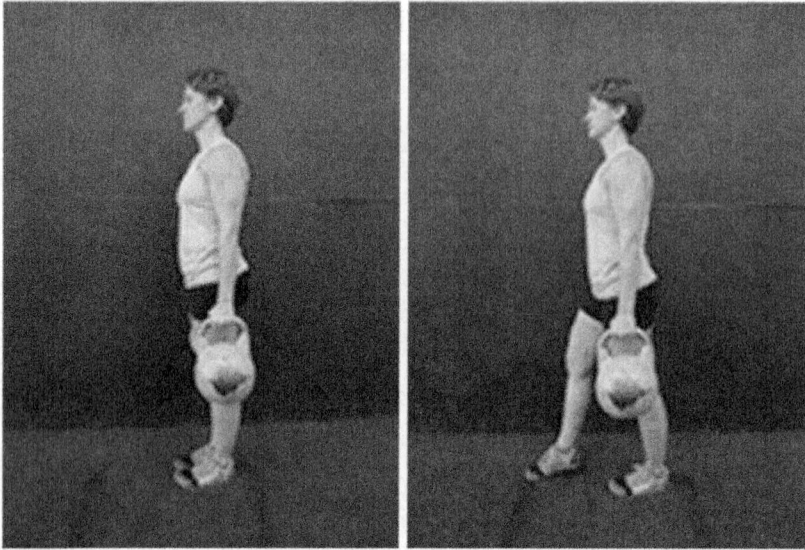

Fast Feet: Start in an athletic stance with feet slightly wider than shoulder width, knees bent. Sprint in place, with minimal leg raise—emphasis on fast feet.

Flutter Kick: Lie on the back with both legs extended. Keeps hands on the ground or anchor them underneath the body. Move legs up and down in a fast swimming motion, alternating legs.

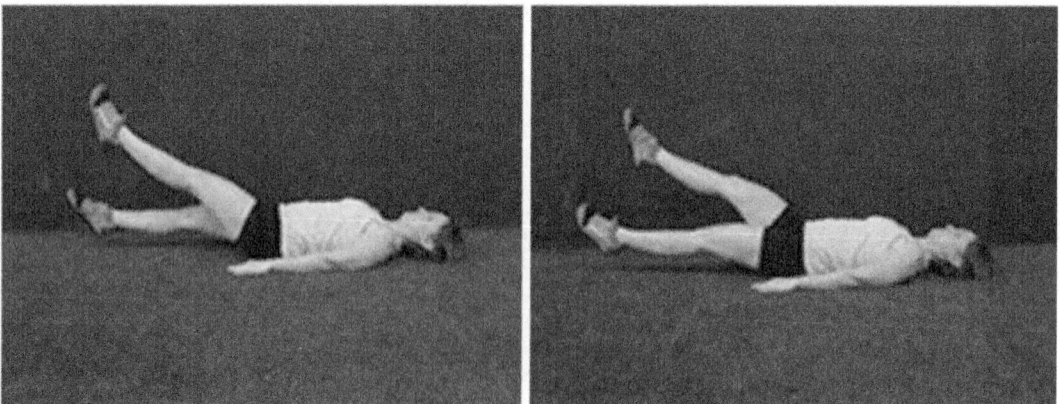

Forward Lunge: Stand with feet together and hands at the waist. Take a big step forward and bend legs to form 90-degree angles. Return to standing by pressing back up with the lead foot. Keep body upright while alternating legs.

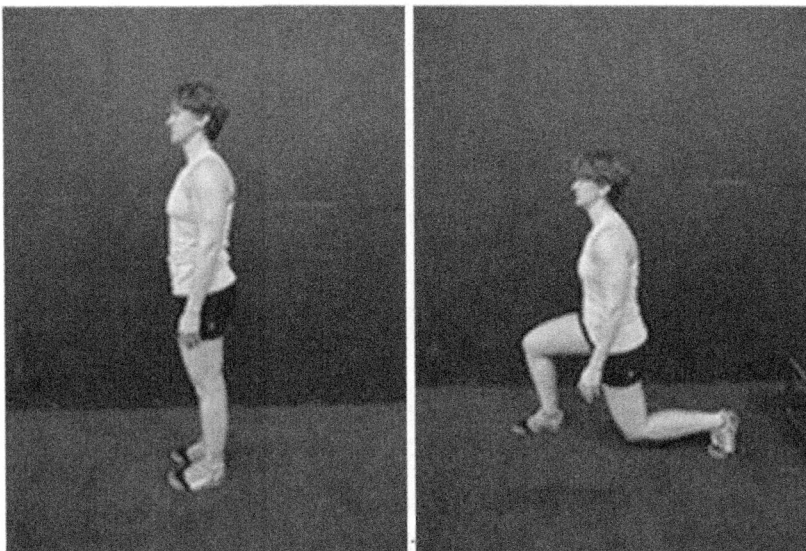

Four Square Jump: Jump in an imaginary square pattern touching each corner of the square with each jump.

Frankensteins: Stand with legs together and both arms extending out in front. Step and kick one leg straight up to the corresponding hand, keeping leg as straight as possible. Try to touch the toe with the hand then return as while stepping forward. Repeat, alternating sides. Keep arms high and be conscious to kick "up" to the hand.

Front-Loaded Reverse Lunge: Hold a barbell in the front rack position—the barbell rests on the collarbones, fingertips resting on the barbell, and elbows pointing straight ahead. Grip should be slightly wider than the shoulders and palms should be facing up. Step one foot back and bend at the knees to go into a reverse lunge. Press back up and repeat on the other leg.

Glute Bridges: Lie on back in a bent-knee position with feet flat on the floor, close to rear. Gently contract abdominal muscles to flatten the low back into the floor. Keep the abdominals engaged, push through the heels and lift the hips up off the floor. Avoid arching the low back. Squeeze glute muscles and slowly lower back to the starting position.

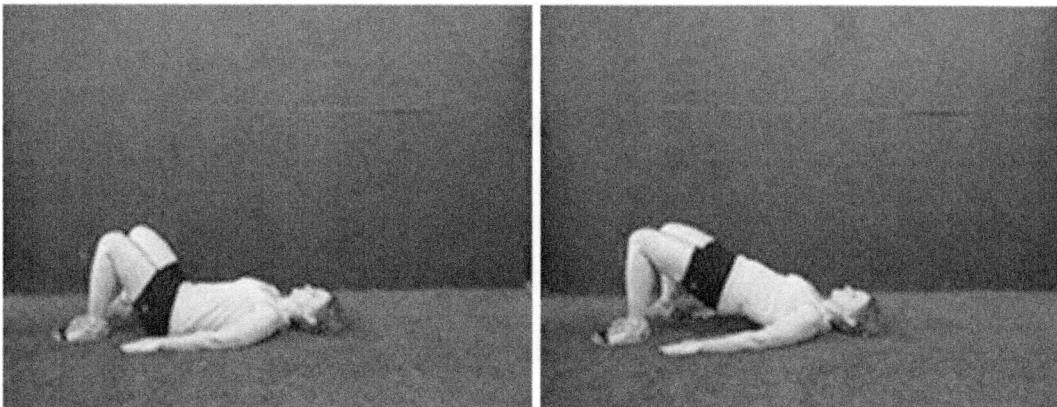

Goblet Squat: Feet slightly wider than shoulder width apart. Hold a kettlebell or dumbbell with both hands right against the chest. Lower yourself into a squat and raise back up to the starting position.

Good Mornings: Stand with feet hip width apart, and place hands at the back of the head with elbows opened wide. Press the butt backward, hinging at the hips, until back is almost parallel to the floor. Keep a slight bend in the knees while bending forward. Return to standing, squeezing the glutes at the top position.

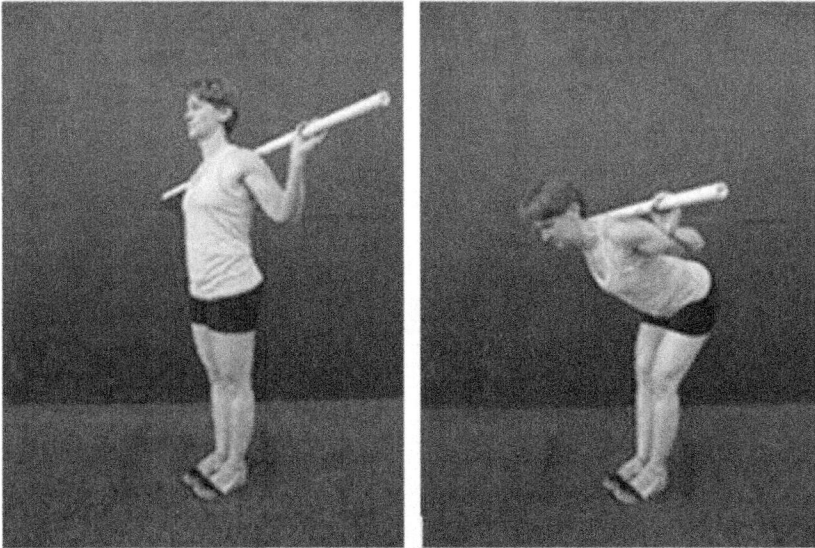

Hammer Curl: Stand upright with arms extended by the sides and a set of dumbbells in both hands. Turn the hands so that the palms are facing the sides of the legs. Bend the elbows, raising the dumbbells up to the shoulders. Squeeze your biceps and pause for one second when the dumbbells are at shoulder level. Slowly reverse the curl to return the weights to your sides. Keep elbows tucked into the sides and avoid swinging body to raise the weight.

Hamstring touch walk: Start standing with both feet hip width apart. Extend one leg in front of you with the heel touching the ground and toe pointing up to the ceiling. Bend forward with your arms held straight and sweep your arms from the forward foot up to the sky while keeping your toes up on your front foot. Repeat the movement, alternating steps.

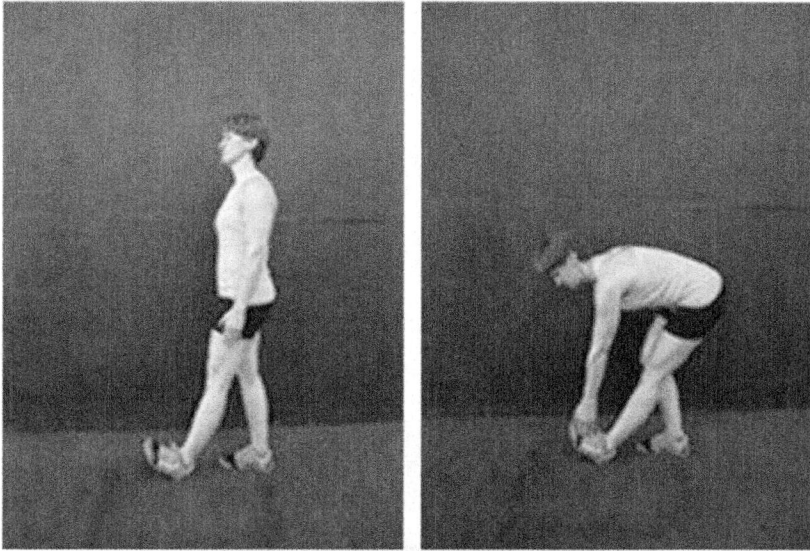

Hand Release Push Ups: Begin in a plank position on both hands. Lower down to the bottom of the push-up position. Once the chest touches the ground, lift both palms off the ground. Push back up to the top of the push-up position. Repeat the movement!

High Knees: Start standing with feet hip width apart. Lift up one knee so that the leg is parallel to the floor. Lightly jog with high knees going to this high parallel position.

High Knee Pulls: Stand with feet hip width apart. Lift and bend a knee, gently pulling it close to the body. Return and repeat while alternating legs.

Hollow Rock: Lie on your back in the hollow body position: lower back in contact with the floor, arms extended close to the ears, and legs extended straight with toes pointed. Begin rocking back and forth maintaining the hollow body form.

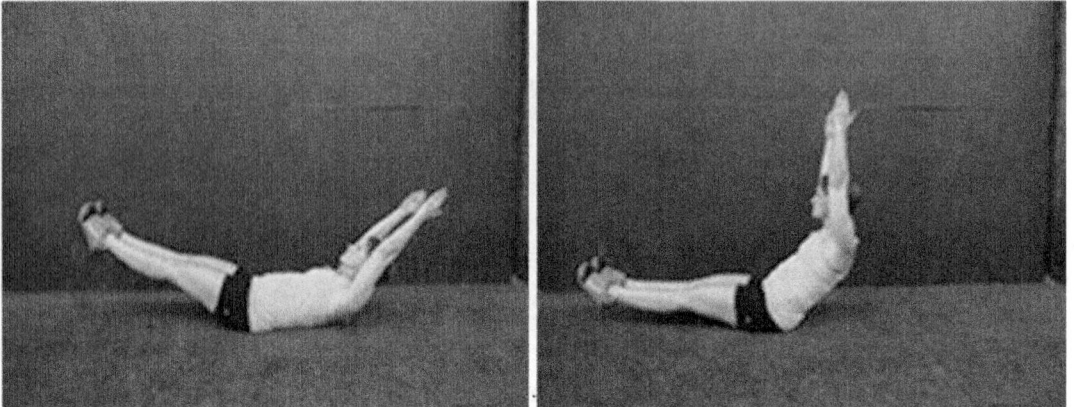

Hollow Rock Hold: Lie on your back in the hollow body position: lower back in contact with the floor, arms extended close to the ears, and legs extended straight with toes pointed. Hold position.

Inchworm: Stand with feel slightly apart and bend forward at the hips. Extend arms in front of the body and walk forward into the top of a push-up position. Then, walk the feet up to meet the hands in front, keeping legs as straight as possible.

Jumping Jacks: Stand tall with arms at the sides. In a fluid motion, jump legs out to the side and raise arms up overhead. Land and repeat.

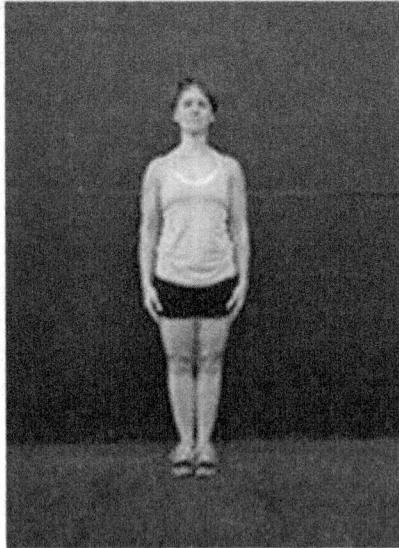

Jumping Lunges: Start standing. Lower down into a lunge, then jump and switch legs rapidly in mid-flight to land with the opposite leg forward. Lower down into another lunge and repeat.

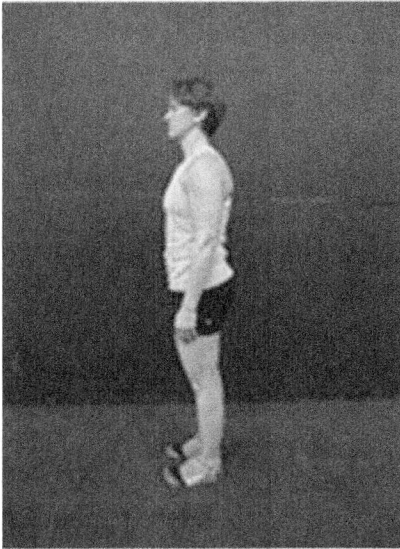

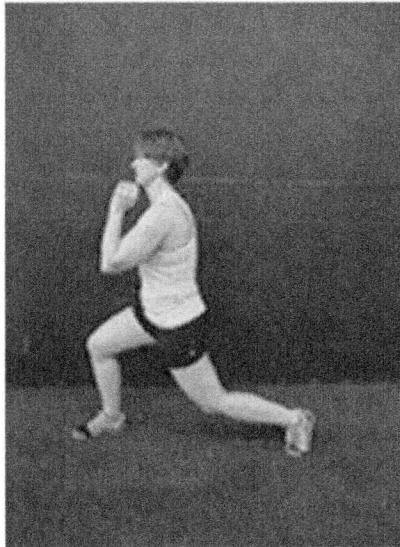

Jump the Line: Imagine a vertical line on the floor to one side. Hop over the line with both feet then hop back to start position as quickly as possible. Repeat.

Jump Touch: Stand close to a wall, extend arm overhead against the wall. Visualize a spot 1 foot above the highest part of the hand. Jump repeatedly and touch that spot.

Junkyard Dog: The junkyard dog is a partner warm-up consist of 2 separate parts. First Part: Partner #1 sits on the floor with arms extended to the side (parallel to the floor) and legs extended out front. Partner #2 starts behind partner #1, jumps over one arm, turns 90 degrees, jumps over legs, turns 90 degrees and jumps over the other arm. Turn 180 degrees and repeat going the opposite direction. Perform this 5 times, then switch. Second Part: Partner #1 gets on his hands and knees curled tightly, and partner #2 jumps over partner #1. Then Partner #1 pikes up and Partner #2 crawls under partner #1. Perform this 5 times, then switch.

Kettlebell Swing: Stand with legs shoulder width apart. Grip a kettlebell, positioned at the feet in between legs. Bend knees and go into a semi-squat, picking up the kettlebell and keeping arms loose. Swing the kettlebell using power thrusts from the hip, thigh and lower back muscles.

Kneeling Push Up: Place hands on the ground, shoulder width apart, both knees on the ground. Lower the torso to the ground until the chest touches the floor. Push back up to the starting position.

Lateral Box Jump: Stand laterally to the side of a cardio step. Jump sideways across the step to the floor on the other side. Jump back over the step in the opposite direction.

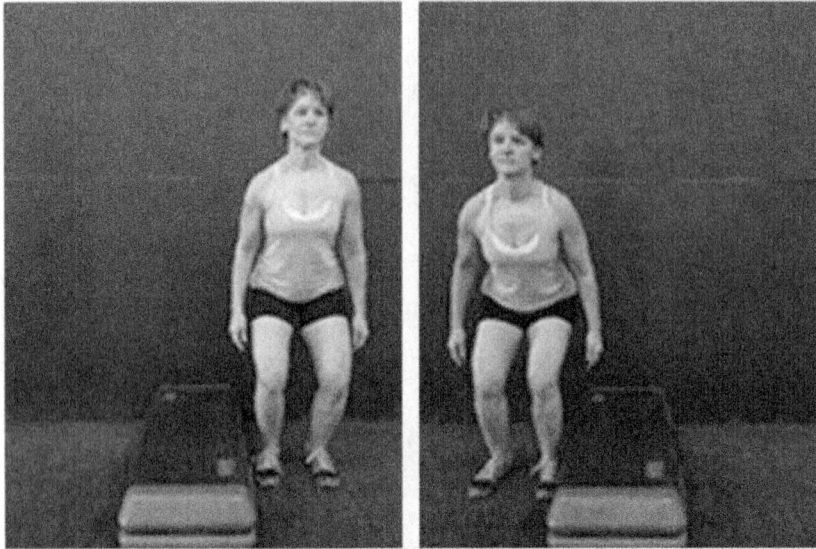

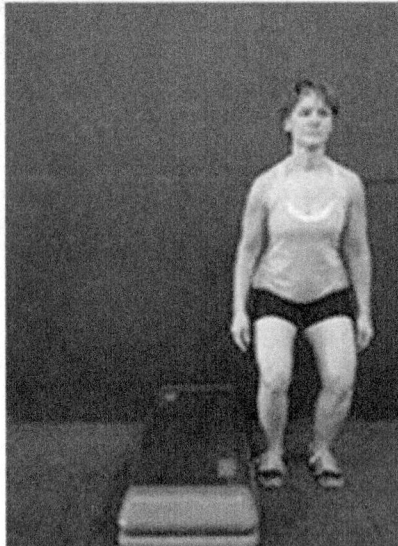

Lateral Walk with Resistance Band: Take resistance band and hold it out in front of you. Now step onto the band with feet hip width apart. Put the bands into the opposite hands. Take a step sideways to the right as far as you can. Actively resist the pull of the exercise band as you bring your left leg slowly toward your right, returning to the starting position.

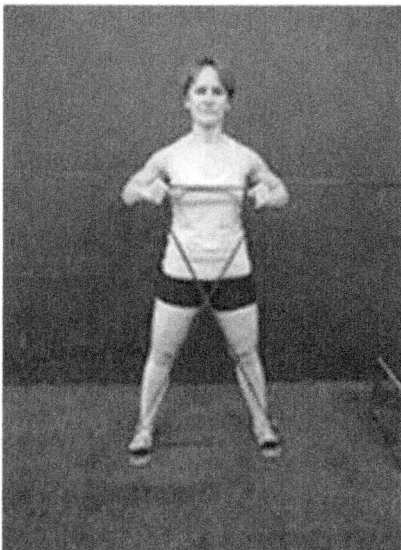

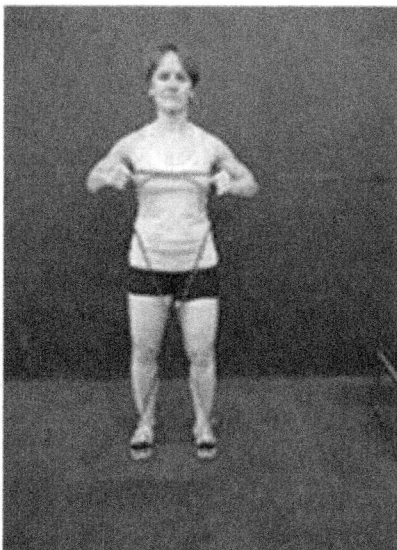

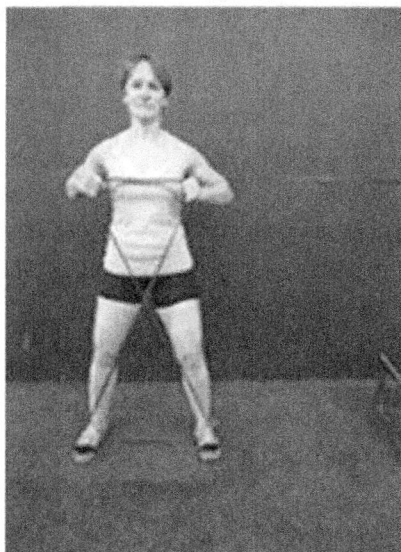

Lunge Hold: Hold at the bottom of a forward lunge, keeping the back knee just barely off the ground.

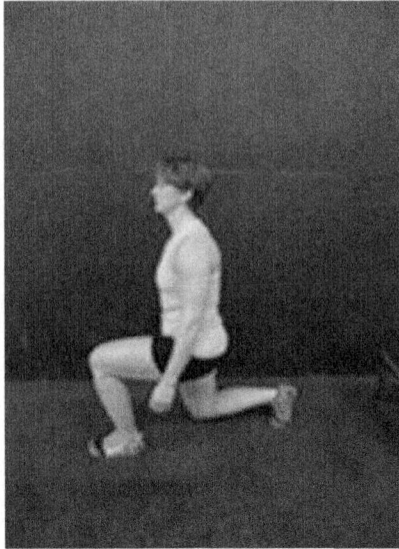

Manmakers: Hold a pair of dumbbells in hand. Squat down, dumbbells by the feet. Kick legs back into a plank position. Perform a push-up, then do a one arm row on each side, bringing elbow up as high as possible. Hop both feet forward to the hands, and rise by cleaning the weights as you hop a second time and land into the bottom of a squat with both dumbbells to the shoulders. Rise up explosively and press the dumbbells overhead. Lower the dumbbells back to your shoulders, then bend over as you squat down to return the weights back to the floor in front of you. Repeat for reps.

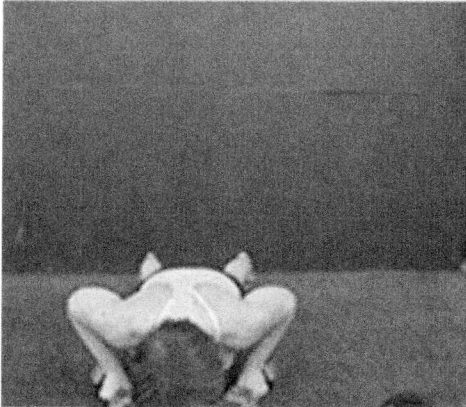

Medicine Ball Chest Pass with Partner: Stand with feet shoulder width apart and a medicine ball in hands at chest height. Stand 5-10 feet from partner. With both hands placed evenly on the ball, quickly push the ball on a straight line away from your chest as forcefully as possible. Catch the ball back from partner.

Medicine Ball Sit-up with Partner: Facing partner, sit on floor with knees bent. Bottoms of feet are pressed together with partner. First individual holds medicine ball with both hands, then lies back with ball overhead and taps ball to floor. Individual throws ball to partner from overhead while sitting up. Partner catches ball slightly above and in front of head and repeats steps. Continue to volley ball back and forth.

Medball Slam: Stand tall with feet shoulder width apart and a medicine ball in hands. Reach the medicine ball high overhead and quickly slam it down. Catch the ball as soon as possible on the way up and repeat the movement.

Monkey Jumps: Stand with a pair of dumbbells. Perform an alternating split jump (jumping lunge) with simultaneous high pull on each jump.

Mountain Climbers: Start in a plank position both hands on the floor. Drive one knee up towards the corresponding elbow and quickly alternate sides. Increase speed to increase your heart rate.

OTM: On The Minute. At the top of each minute, perform the assigned movement or exercise.

Plank: Lie on stomach with toes pressing into the floor. Press up onto the forearms on the ground and lift the body into a straight line. Hold.

Plank Jacks: Start in a plank position on the hands with feet together. Hop feet out about 2 feet and back in. Repeat.

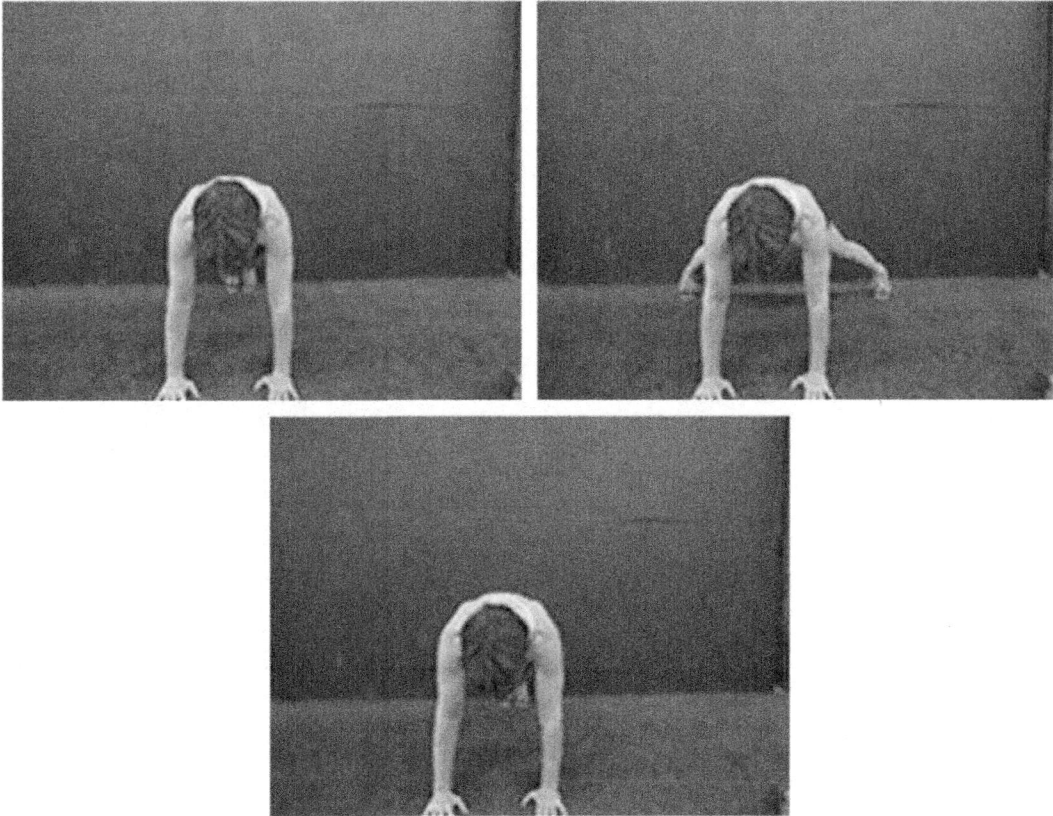

Plank Up-Downs: Start in the high plank position with both hands on the ground. Slowly lower onto the left forearm, and then lower to the right forearm. Then slowly raise back onto the right hand, then raise onto the left hand. Keep hips as square as possible to the ground and try to keep the body from moving.

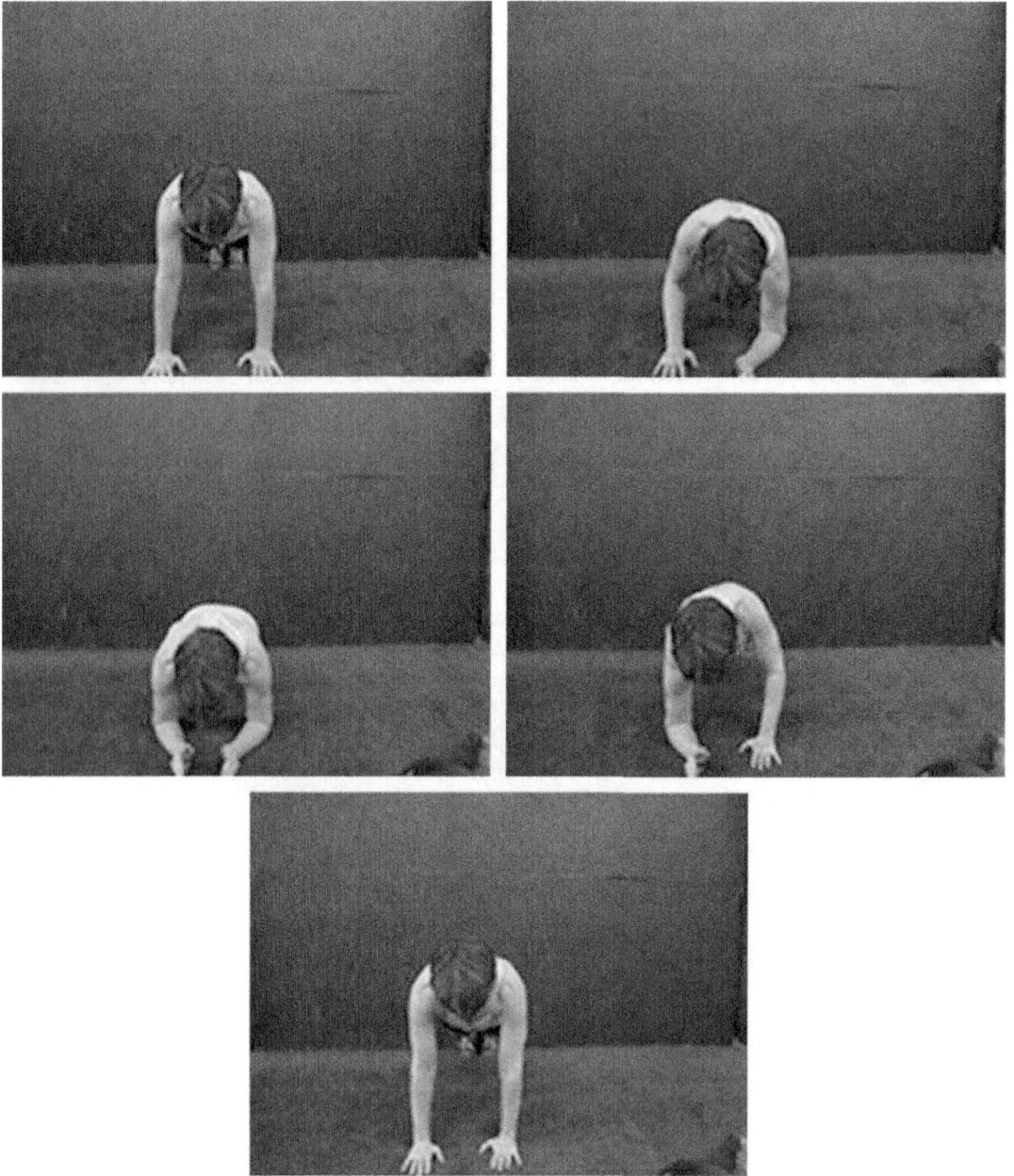

Plank with Shoulder Tap: Start in the high or low plank position, either both hands or both forearms on the ground. Lift up one hand to touch your opposite shoulder and return to the start position. Alternate arms. Keep the hips as square as possible to the ground and try to keep the body from moving.

Plank Walkout with Push-up: Stand with feel slightly apart and bend forward at the hips. Extend arms in front of the body and walk forward into the top of a push-up position. Perform a push-up and walk back up to standing position.

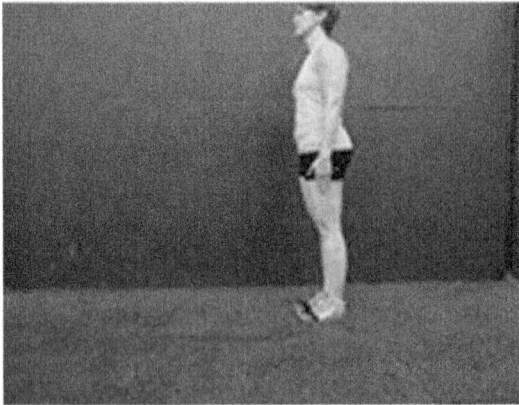 

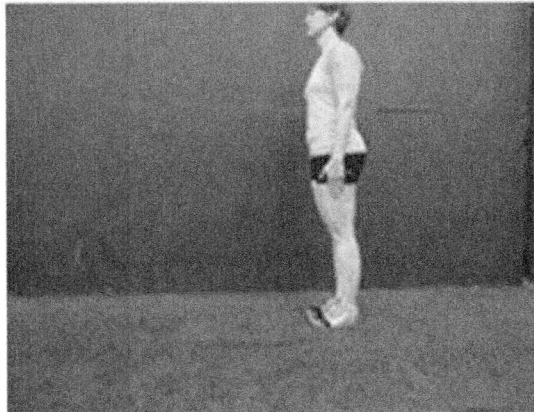

Prisoner Walk: Start in a deep squat position with hands clasped behind the head. Waddle forward one leg at a time in that squat position.

Push-ups: Start in a plank position, hands on the floor with arms straight and hands directly under shoulders. Squeeze glutes tight, and lower the torso until chest hits the ground and push back up. Keep the neck neutral and elbows close to torso.

Rear Loaded Forward Lunge: Load a barbell/bodypump bar behind head on shoulders. Lunge forward to one knee.

Renegade Row: With dumbbells in hand, prop yourself up to plank position. Perform a push up. Row the right dumbbell, lower it back to the floor and row the left dumbbell. Make sure the hips stay parallel to the floor without rotating. One Renegade Row is push-up/row/row. Some class members might choose to push-up/row right/push-up/row left.

Reverse Lunge: Start with feet together. Step one foot back and bend at the knees until rear knee touches the ground. Keep chest up. Press back up and repeat on the other leg.

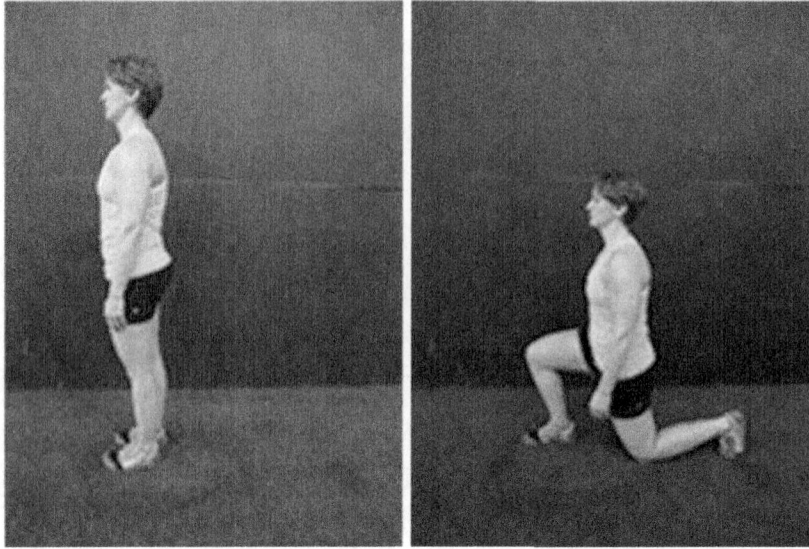

Runner's Lunge: Start in an upper plank position. Lift and place the right foot to the outside of the right hand and hold the deep stretch for one count before returning to the plank position. Repeat on the opposite side and continue to alternate. Keep the back knee off the ground.

Russian Twist: Sit with good posture with knees slightly bent and heels just off the floor. Hold a dumbbell in front of the chest. Lean back slightly to engage the abs. Twist the torso from side-to-side, tapping the weight on the floor on each side, keeping the heels off the ground.

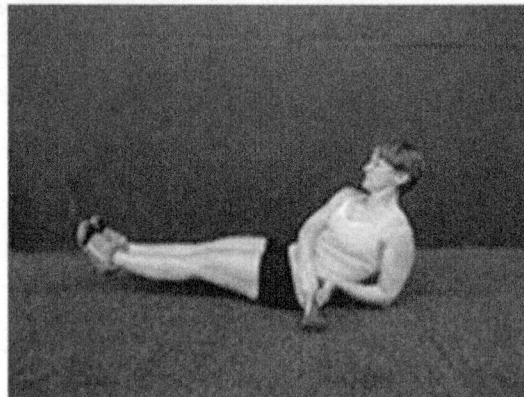

Side Plank: Lying on one side, place elbow on the floor directly underneath your shoulder. Pile feet on top of each other. Activating core, lift entire body up in alignment to neutral.

Side Plank Gravedigger: Begin in side plank position. Lift free arm and tuck fingers behind the ear. Rotate top shoulder forward lowering the elbow towards the ground. Keep rotating until elbow touches the ground. Return back to the starting position.

Side Shuffle: Start with bent knees in partial squat, hands held in front of chest. Shuffle briskly from side to side keeping body low and chest lifted.

Sit-ups: Lie on back with knees bent with feet flat on the floor or the bottoms of feet touching, arms extended behind the head and hands touching the floor directly behind the head. Squeeze shoulder blades together. Brace abs and then raise the body up towards the knees, shoulders should be lifted off the floor. Keep head in line with your spine, tilting the chin forward slightly. Touch the floor in front of the feet then reverse and slowly roll back down to the starting position.

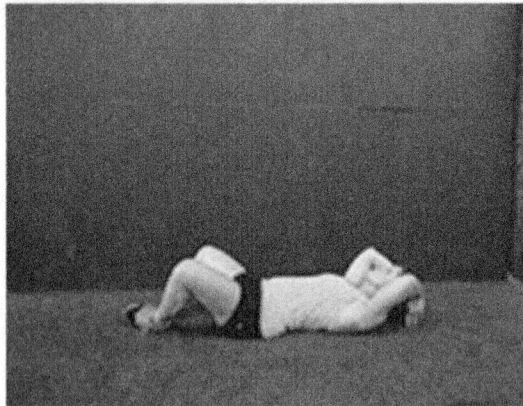

Spiderman Crawl: Start in the Runner's Lunge position. Bring one hand forward while dragging the opposite leg forward until that knee comes to the forward elbow. Repeat the movement with the opposite hand and opposite leg in order to gradually move forward.

Split Squat: Start standing with both feet together. Take a large step backwards and stand on the ball of the back foot with the heel off the ground and the front foot flat. Drop back knee straight down just above the floor and return back to start position while squeezing the glutes.

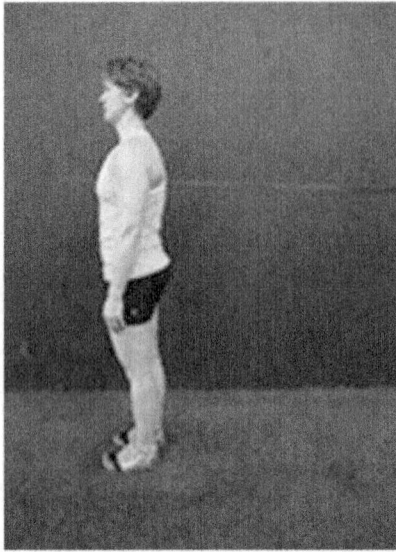

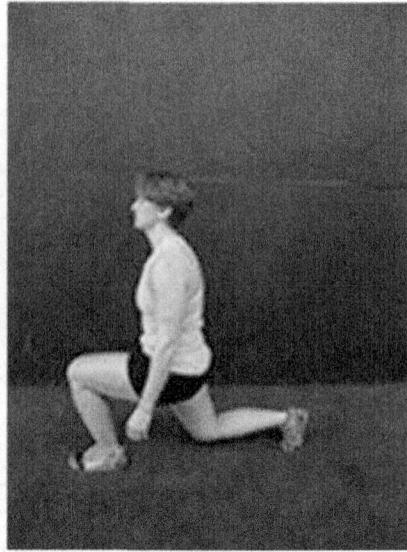

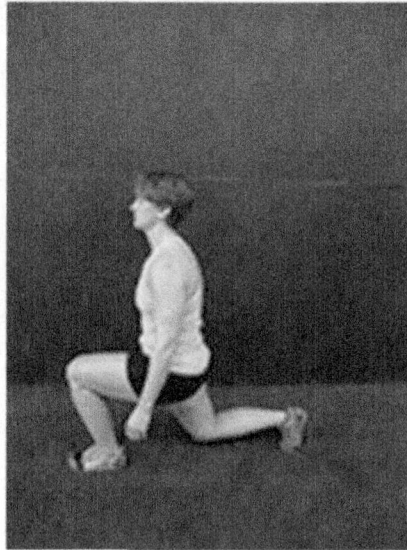

Squat Hold: Stand with feet hip width apart. Sit hips back and down into a squat position and hold.

Squat Jacks: Standing with feet close together and hands clasped behind the head, push hips back to get into a half-squat position. Jump the feet out to the sides, maintaining the squat position. Quickly jump feet back to the starting position.

Squat Jump: Stand with feet hip width apart. Sit hips back and down into a squat position. Jump straight up into the air and land softly back into the squat position. Repeat.

Squat to Stand: Stand tall with feet about shoulder width apart from each other. Then, push your hips back, bend at your waist, and grab your toes. Drop hips back into a squat and lift the chest upward while lowering the body towards the floor. Hold then push the hips upward to a standing position while continuing to hold toes.

180 Squat Jumps: Stand with feet hip width apart. Sit hips back and down into a squat position. Explode out of the squat while rotating the entire body 180 degrees and landing softly in a squat facing the opposite direction. Repeat and change directions.

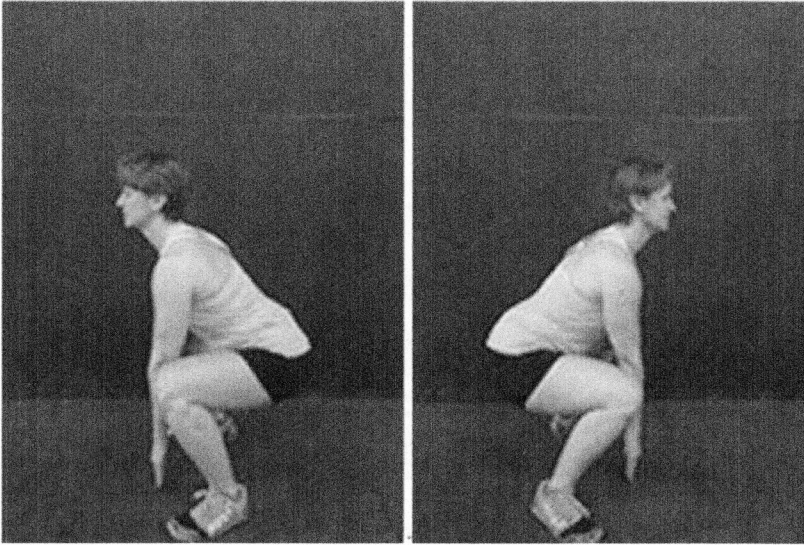

Squat Pulse: Stand with feet hip width apart. Sit hips back and down into a squat position. Hold it at the bottom as you pulse a few inches up and down.

Standing Quad Stretch: Stand on one leg with knees touching. Grab foot with the corresponding hand and pull toward the butt. Keep chest upright.

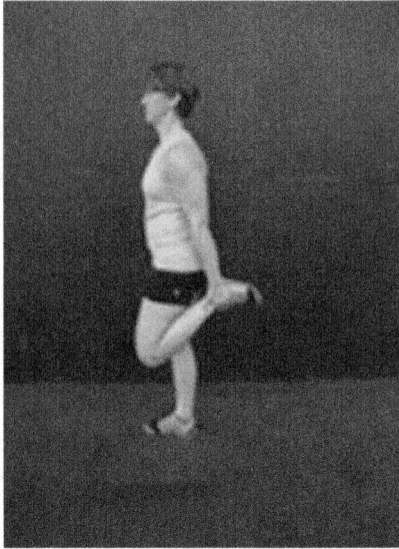

Standing Scissor Kick: Stand upright, feet shoulder width apart. Jump feet forward and back in a scissor motion.

Step Ups: (See Dumbbell Step Up)

Suicides: Set up 4 cones an equal distance apart in a straight line. Get in a sprint-ready stance at the first cone. Sprint from cone 1 to cone 2, touch the ground and quickly change direction and sprint back to cone 1. Touch the ground, sprint to cone 3, touch the ground, sprint back to cone 1. Touch the ground, sprint to cone 4, touch the ground and sprint back to cone 1.

Supermans: Lie on stomach with toes pointed down and arms stretched out overhead. Squeeze glutes and slowly lift knees and arms up and down simultaneously.

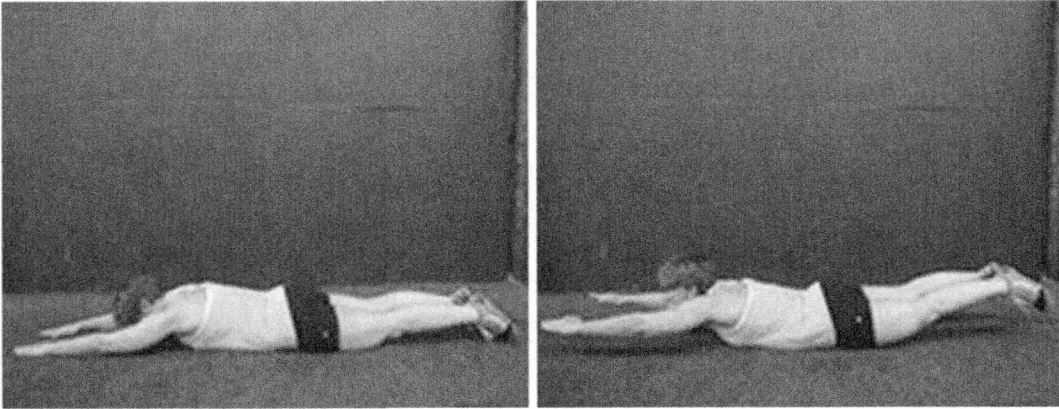

T-Push-up: Start in a plank position, with hands on the floor with arms straight and hands directly under shoulders. Squeeze glutes tight, and lower the torso until chest hits the ground and push back up. Lift one arm from the floor and raise towards the ceiling while twisting the torso to that side. Roll onto the sides of the feet and keep the body straight. Return to the starting position. Repeat raising the opposite arm to complete the set.

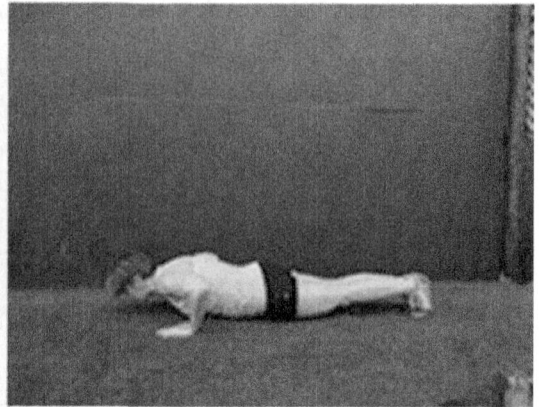

Tabata: A work-rest method. For 20 seconds, complete as many reps of a given exercise as possible. Rest for 10 seconds and repeat this seven more times for a total of eight intervals. This will equal 4 minutes.

Thruster: (See Dumbbell Thruster)

Tuck Jump: Stand with feet slightly inside the width of the shoulders. Bend the knees slightly. Explode into the air and bring the knees up as high as possible in a tucked position. Repeat for the required number of repetitions.

V Hold: Lie on back with arms overhead. Lift arms, shoulders and legs off the ground in a "V" position and hold.

V-Up: Lie flat the back on the floor with arms extended straight back behind the head. Bend at the waist while simultaneously raising the legs and arms to meet in a jackknife position. Reach towards the raised feet while maintaining the "V" shape. Lower arms and legs back to the starting position.

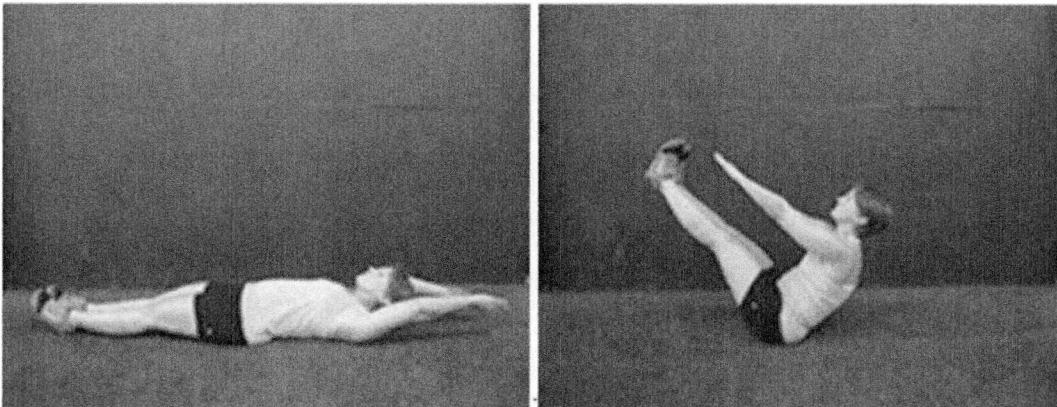

Walking Lunges: Stand with feet together and hands at the waist. Take a big step forward and bend legs to form a 90-degree angles.

Step feet together by bringing back foot to front foot. Step forward with the opposite leg and continue. Keep body upright while alternating legs.

Walking Lunges with Torso Twist: Stand with feet together and hands at the waist. Take a big step forward and bend legs to form a

90-degree angles. From the torso, twist to the right or left with a slow controlled movement.

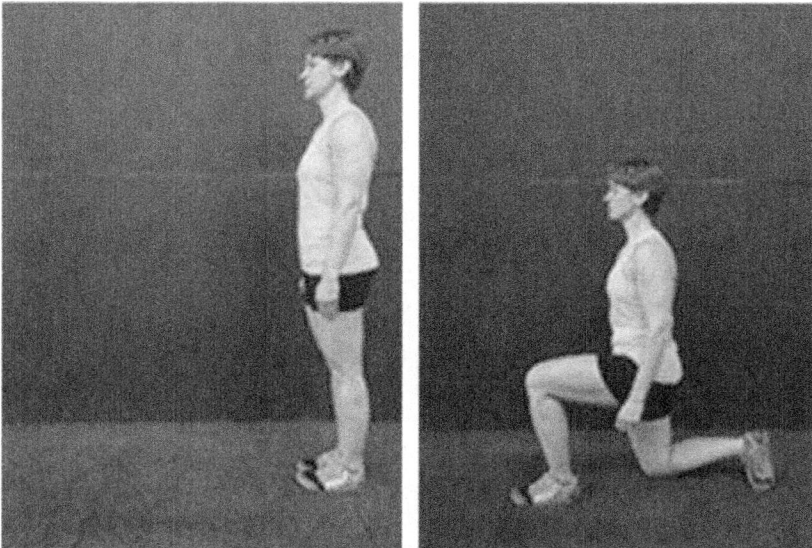

Wall Sit: Sit back against a wall with legs at a 90-degree angle. Keep abs tight and small of the back pressed into the wall. Hold.add

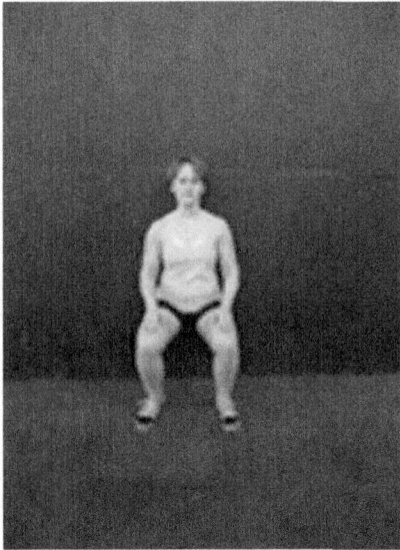

Weighted Sit-up: Perform a sit-up holding a DB to the chest.

Weighted Squat Jump: Hold a dumbbell vertically by the top knob, with arms extended and elbows unbent. Stand with a slight bend in knees, chest up and feet hip width apart. Sit hips back and down into a squat position, just until the bottom of the dumbbell touches the ground. Jump up explosively, keeping chest high and facing forward, and keeping arms extended straight down. Land softly in the bottom position and repeat.

Final Words

Writing a book is a journey that calls for perseverance, hard effort, and the support and encouragement of many people. I'm thankful to everyone who helped make this book possible because it's been both a difficult and rewarding experience to complete.

First of all, I want to say thank you to all the people who have shared their life stories with me. The personal experiences and insights shared have been the book's heart and soul, from those by family members, friends, and study participants who kindly gave their time and perspectives.

I am also incredibly appreciative of all the people who offered constructive criticism on the draft throughout the writing process. My ideas have been strengthened, my arguments have been made clearer, and my writing has improved thanks to their observations, advice, and criticism. I am lucky to have such a supportive and talented network of people in my life because the advice from coworkers, mentors, and fellow writers has been priceless.

In addition, I want to thank the research community for its important efforts. This work's foundation was laid by the theories, knowledge, and methodologies created by academics and researchers in a variety of disciplines, and I am grateful for their commitment to furthering understanding and knowledge.

I also want to express my gratitude to my publication team for their assistance. Their efforts were crucial in realizing this work, from the acquisition editor who saw the potential in this book to the production team who toiled diligently to make sure the finished product met the highest standards of quality. I appreciate having the chance to work with such a creative and encouraging team, and my editor's advice, criticism, and encouragement have been especially helpful.

I also want to thank my family and friends, who have been a constant source of encouragement and support for me throughout this path. The hardest times haven't stopped me because of their unflinching faith in me and my capabilities. I am also appreciative of my family's tolerance and understanding during the extended weekends and long hours I spent writing and studying.

Finally, I'd like to express my gratitude to the book's fans for their support of my writing. The thought that my words and ideas might affect how people think and act is humbling because writing can be a solitary and introspective process. With this work, I want to encourage readers to think about their own experiences, challenge their preconceptions, and interact with the world in a kind and inquisitive way.

As a result of a team endeavor involving the contributions of numerous people, a book can only be finished with their combined efforts. I am appreciative of the support, advice, and input that my family, loved ones, study participants, reviewers, researchers, publishing team, and readers have provided for this work. I appreciate you coming along for the ride.

Charlottew R Stephensh

Printed in Great Britain
by Amazon